"Scholars and lay people alike will find these previously unpublished sermons on the parable of the Net, delivered towards the end of the Great Awakening, a rich resource for learning more about Edwards's mature view on true religious experience. The introductions help the reader appreciate the historical context and Edwards's unique style. While this series has been overshadowed in the past by Religious Affections, the reader will value their simplicity, beauty, and enduring biblical truths."

—Karin Spiecker Stetina,
author of *Jonathan Edwards' Early Understanding of Religious Experience*

"Often overlooked, Matthew's gospel is a resource the church can't afford to neglect. We can be thankful then to the Jonathan Edwards Center at Yale for publishing for the first time Edwards's sermons on the parable of the Net. They provide a fine introduction to Edwards's skills in preaching, and pithy summaries of his theological priorities. We find here the big ideas of the *Religious Affections*, but preached in direct and simple language."

—Rhys Bezzant,
Director of the Jonathan Edwards Center in Australia

Sermons by Jonathan Edwards on the Matthean Parables
volume III

*Drawing in the Net,* by Jan Luyken

Sermons by Jonathan Edwards on the Matthean Parables
VOLUME III

FISH OUT OF THEIR ELEMENT
(ON THE PARABLE OF THE NET)

EDITED BY
Kenneth P. Minkema and Adriaan C. Neele

WITH AN INTRODUCTION BY
Wilson H. Kimnach

CASCADE *Books* • Eugene, Oregon

The *Jonathan Edwards*
Center at Yale University

SERMONS BY JONATHAN EDWARDS ON THE MATTHEAN PARABLES,
VOLUME III
Fish Out of Their Element (On the Parable of the Net)

Cascade Books
A Division of Wipf and Stock Publishers
199 W. 8th Ave., Suite 3
Eugene, OR 97401

www.wipfandstock.com

ISBN 13: 978-1-61097-716-6

*Cataloging-in-Publication data:*

Edwards, Jonathan, 1703–1758.

    Sermons from Jonathan Edwards on the Matthean parables, volume III : fish out of their element (on the parable of the net) / Jonathan Edwards, edited by Kenneth P. Minkema and Adriaan C. Neele with an introduction by Wilson H. Kimnach.

    x + 90 p. ; 23 cm. Includes bibliographical references and index.

    ISBN 13: 978-1-61097-716-6

    1. Sermons of Jonathan Edwards / Jonathan Edwards. 2. Jesus Christ—Parables. 3. Bible. N.T. Matthew—Criticism, interpretation, etc. 4. Preaching—United States—History—18th century. I. Kimnach, Wilson H. II. Minkema, Kenneth P. III. Neele, Adriaan C. IV. Title.

BX7233.E42 M25 2012

Manufactured in the U.S.A.

# CONTENTS

# LIST OF ILLUSTRATIONS

# LIST OF CONTRIBUTORS

**Dr. Wilson H. Kimnach** is the Presidential Professor in the Humanities (Emeritus), Bridgeport University, and General Sermon Editor of *The Works of Jonathan Edwards.*

**Dr. Kenneth P. Minkema** is the Executive Editor and Director of the Jonathan Edwards Center, Yale University, and Research Scholar at Yale Divinity School.

**Rev. Dr. Adriaan C. Neele** is the Associate Editor and Director of the Jonathan Edwards Center, Yale University, Research Scholar at Yale Divinity School, and Professor Extraordinary at the University of the Free State, Bloemfontein, South Africa.

# PREFACE

THIS THIRD VOLUME OF *SERMONS BY JONATHAN EDWARDS ON THE Matthean Parables* contains a previously unpublished series of sermons by Edwards on Jesus' Parable of the Net, as found in Matthew 13. Edwards preached these sermons in 1746, after the major phase of the Great Awakening had passed in New England and during the very months he was completing and publishing *A Treatise Concerning Religious Affections*, his masterful statement on the true and false signs of true grace. Therefore, this series is significant for its place in Edwards' rich and evolving view of the nature of religious experience. To assist the reader, preceding the series are two introductions that describe Edwards' preaching style and method, and provide an historical context.

## A NOTE ON EDWARDS' TEXT

Edwards' sermon series, *Fish Out of Their Element*, is printed here in full from the original manuscripts as transcribed and edited by the staff of the Jonathan Edwards Center at Yale University. In presenting these texts, the editors have followed the conventions of the Yale Edition of *The Works of Jonathan Edwards* (26 volumes, 1957–2008), regularizing spelling, capitalization, and format. Preserved here are Edwards' own words, punctuated in an eighteenth-century style. Because the manuscript was largely uncorrected by Edwards—it was, after all, for his personal use for public delivery—there are inconsistencies in number, style, and tense, which, as a rule, are left as they are; any changes are footnoted. In any given manuscript there are a great number of deletions, so here only deletions of significant textual importance are footnoted. Readers may find Edwards' manner of writing challenging at first, but we believe the effort to understand Edwards in his own terms, in his own idiom, and to get a sense of the immediacy of his preaching, will be rewarded. Finally, Scripture quotes are rendered according to the King James Bible, which was the version Edwards used.

One feature of the text presented below bears special explanation: cases of editorial interpolation, which become particularly important in Edwards' later sermons, in which he increasingly resorted to outlines and fragmentary statements. For this reason, some of the sermons in this series may seem short, but it is important to bear in mind that Edwards would have extemporized on any given point. Editorial interpolations are of two types. First, outright omissions by Edwards, and lacunae in the manuscript, are filled by insertions in square brackets ([,]). Secondly, one aspect of the outlinish nature of this sermon series is easily seen in the many dashes of varying lengths that Edwards drew at the beginning, in the middle, and at the end of statements. These dashes represent repeated words or phrases, as well as connective pieces of sentences, which Edwards would have provided extemporaneously. Where these dashes have been editorially amplified, they are surrounded by curly brackets ({,}).

The manuscripts are in the Edwards Collection, Beinecke Rare Book and Manuscript Library, Yale University. The manuscript is in eight duodecimo booklets, composed of different kinds of paper and of scraps, including foolscap (usually as outside covers for booklets), fan paper, and discarded prayer bids and marriage banns. There are several lacunae within the booklets, which are detailed in the annotations. Transcripts can be viewed at edwards.yale.edu. The introduction by Wilson H. Kimnach is excerpted from his larger discussion of "Jonathan Edwards' Art of Prophesying" in *The Works of Jonathan Edwards, 10, Sermons and Discourses, 1720–1723* (New Haven, Yale University Press, 1990), 21–27, 36–42.

# INTRODUCTION
## Edwards the Preacher

Wilson H. Kimnach

### EDWARDS' THOUGHTS ON PREACHING

JONATHAN EDWARDS WAS IN FULL AGREEMENT WITH HIS TEACHERS RE-
specting the exalted status of the preacher. For though his writings
occasionally contain references to "earthen vessels" and sometimes em-
phasize the preacher's humble situation as a son of Adam, it is much
more common for Edwards to see the preacher as a man exalted and
even transfigured by his calling. Indeed, in some of the earliest entries
in his "Miscellanies" (nos. mm, qq, and 40) Edwards attempts to define
to his own satisfaction the nature of the call, the limits and quality of a
minister's influence in society, and the power in preaching or teaching
the divine Word.

> Yet it is clear that those that are in the New Testament called min-
> isters are not every private Christian, and consequently if [any]
> such remain now as are there spoken of, they are distinct from
> other Christians. 'Tis clear they are born undistinguished; from
> this 'tis clear they are distinguished afterwards. 'Tis also evident
> that they are distinguished some way or other by Christ . . .[1]

---

1. "Miscellanies" no. *mm*, in *Works of Jonathan Edwards, 13, "Miscellanies," a-500*,
edited by Thomas A. Schafer (New Haven: Yale University Press, 1994), 187. After initial citation, volumes in *The Works of Jonathan Edwards* (New Haven: Yale University
Press, 1957–2008) will be referred to as "WJE" plus volume and page numbers. Texts
by JE published in the Jonathan Edwards Center's website (edwards.yale.edu) will be
referred to as "WJEO" plus the volume number.

This earliest entry on the office of the preacher calls attention to the essentially aristocratic bias of Edwards, which is quite in keeping with his upbringing, while it also demonstrates his characteristic propensity to rethink every important aspect of his life "from the ground up," regardless of his background and training. He may not seriously question the assumptions of his heritage, but he will insist upon a personal formulation of that heritage in his own written words.

The preacher is, then, a "chosen one" with a distinct charisma as a result of his call to serve Christ. He is invested with a capacity and right to instruct, lead, and judge his people;[2] he has no pretension to civil authority, but in the all-important moral and spiritual realms he is, of all human beings, supremely authoritative. "Miscellanies" no. 40 contains early speculations upon the powers that would inhere in the effective preaching of the Word, specifically:

> Without doubt, ministers are to teach men what Christ would have them to do, and to teach them who doth these things and who doth them not; that is, who are Christians and who are not . . .
>
> Thus, if I in a right manner am become the teacher of a people, so far as they ought to hear what I teach them, so much power I have. Thus, if they are obliged to hear me only because they themselves have chosen me to guide them, and therein declared that they thought me sufficiently instructed in the mind of Christ to teach them, and because I have the other requisites of being their teacher, then I have power as other ministers have in these days. But if it was plain to them that I was under the infallible guidance of Christ, then I should have more power. And if it was plain to all the world of Christians that I was under the infallible guidance of Christ, and [that] I was sent forth to teach the world the will of Christ, then I should have power in all the world. I should have power to teach them what they ought to do, and they would be obliged to hear me; I should have power to teach them who were Christians and who not, and in this likewise they would be obliged to hear me.[3]

As in a daydream, the student-preacher toys with the mystery of the call, and at least by implication ponders the limits and possibilities of the role of a preacher. Could he command the people, or even the

2. WJE 13:188.
3. WJE 13:222.

world, as a divine messenger? Obviously, there must be some immediate sign, some quality of utterance, that would in itself attest to the supernatural ordination. In this early passage Edwards is already pondering aspects of sermonic style, but characteristically he begins on the most general and profound, most philosophical level. Puritan ministers had always been urged to "preach powerfully," but in this meditation there are new undertones, and "power" clearly relates to a divine investiture that transcends conventional sectarian sanctions. Certainly it seems that Edwards was as well fitted to study the art of preaching under the imperious Solomon Stoddard—his grandfather and predecessor as the pastor of Northampton, Massachusetts—as any man.

Edwards did not pretend to eloquence or a fine style. Indeed, from the first he seems to have made a point of proclaiming his lack of a fine style.

> [T]he practical discourses that follow . . . now appear in that very plain and unpolished dress in which they were first prepared and delivered; which was mostly at a time when the circumstances of the auditory they were preached to, were enough to make a minister neglect, forget, and despise such ornaments as politeness and modishness of style and method, when coming as a messenger from God to souls deeply impressed with a sense of their danger of God's everlasting wrath, to treat with them about their eternal salvation. However unable I am to preach or write politely, if I would, yet I have this to comfort me under such a defect; that God has showed us that he don't need such talents in men to carry on his own work, and that he has been pleased to smile upon and bless a very plain, unfashionable way of preaching. And have we not reason to think that it ever has been, and ever will be, God's manner to bless the foolishness of preaching to save them that believe, let the elegance of language, and excellency of style, be carried to never so great a height, by the learning and wit of the present and future ages?

This passage, from the Preface to *Discourses on Various Important Subjects* (1738),[4] is characteristic of the tone of most of Edwards' prefaces, though the discussion is a little more explicit and fully developed. It is defensive, condemning wit and style out of hand as irrelevant to

---

4. P. v; *The Works of Jonathan Edwards, 19, Sermons and Discourses, 1734–1738*, edited by M. X. Lesser (New Haven: Yale University Press, 2001), 797.

effective preaching, while also suggesting an incapacity for stylistic excellence on his own part.

Part of this may be explained by Edwards' cultural background that would have taught him to think of rhetoric or eloquence as a thing separable from the logical structure of an argument.[5] Since he was consciously developing a heart-piercing manner of writing that would be as spare and efficient as an arrow, he assumed that "style," being an adventitious decoration, would have to be left out. It would not have struck Edwards that that efficacious verbal expression for which he constantly strove and "style" might be the same thing. Thus he really could spend much of his lifetime studying the theory and practice of language and metaphor without "paying any attention to style." Of course, part of the problem is also that, as in the seventeenth century, preaching styles were associated with theological positions. In Edwards' day many of the most eloquent preachers of the East were suspect in Edwards' eyes of being rationalist, Arminian, or just theologically jejune. He would therefore rather deny excellence in his carefully wrought sermons than be thought—perhaps even by himself—to be a creature of wit and style. He was too serious, too full of thought, and too honest for *style*.

Indeed, if Edwards claimed brilliance of any kind it was the more essential and "substantial" excellence of thought, and once again he saw himself as being out of tune with the times:

5. The peculiar attitude that assumes substance and expression to be distinct and separable was quite widespread in the seventeenth century and occasioned the birth of the "plain style" among preachers and "mathematical plainness" in the Royal Society. While a detailed survey of this significant aspect of JE's cultural background is beyond the scope of this introduction, it should be stated that the crucial factor in that background seems to have been the philosophy of Peter Ramus. With the aid of his colleague, Omer Talon, Ramus devised a new formulation of the relationship between logic and rhetoric, involving the transfer of the classical (Ciceronian) invention, disposition, and memory from the province of rhetoric to that of dialectic. This left only style, apprehended as a matter of figures and tropes, and delivery to rhetoric; rhetoric became the sideshow to thought, a crowd-pleasing (or even crowd-deluding) device. Thus, those who were intent upon the intellectual substance of their expression or were intensely earnest, such as Puritan preachers and the new scientists, tended to condemn and avoid "style" as something adventitious and frivolous. Moreover, those who cultivated rhetoric during the seventeenth century actually did tend to artificiality and ornateness, as might be expected when figures and tropes are seen more or less as ends in themselves. For a detailed discussion of the history behind JE's attitude, and an investigation of the long groping toward what we should today call an organic style, see Wilbur S. Howell's *Logic and Rhetoric in England, 1500–1700* (Princeton: Princeton University Press, 1956).

> Our discovering the absurdity of the impertinent and abstruse
> distinctions of the School Divines, may justly give us a distaste
> of such distinctions as have a show of learning in obscure words,
> but convey no light to the mind; but I can see no reason why we
> should also discard those that are clear and rational, and can be
> made out to have their foundation in truth.

In the same Preface,[6] in a sustained argument of two pages, he defends
the virtue of "real" fine distinctions in elaborating the "mysteries" of religion. If, as Cotton Mather contended in *Manuductio ad Ministerium*
(1726), his instruction manual for aspiring ministers, that reason is natural to the soul of man, then Edwards would have him test this capacity,
as he would fully exercise the heart, in the quest of a valid apprehension
of divine truths.

Edwards may have been inspired by the example of his father
Timothy Edwards, minister of East Windsor, Connecticut, to use the utmost rigor in making convicting arguments, and Stoddard undoubtedly
provided the pattern for a potent, "psychological" rhetoric for which
Edwards had no name. But having a finer mind and more imagination
than either Stoddard or Timothy Edwards, Edwards outperformed each
at his specialty while combining elements of both their strategies. His
intense interest in the mysterious power of language, however, was apparently innate.

Edwards' matured vision of the ideal preacher is most completely
delineated in his ordination sermon on John 5:35, entitled *The True
Excellency of a Minister of the Gospel* (1744).[7] There, he insists that a
minister must be "both a burning and a shining light"; that "his heart
burn with love to Christ, and fervent desires of the advancement of his
kingdom and glory," and that "his instructions [be] clear and plain, ac-
commodated to the capacity of his hearers, and tending to convey light
to their understandings." This peculiar combination of head and heart,
he insists, is absolutely necessary to the success of a preacher:

> When light and heat are thus united in a minister of the gospel,
> it shows that each is genuine, and of a right kind, and that both
> are divine. Divine light is attended with heat; and so, on the other

6. P. iii; WJE 19:795–96.

7. *The Works of Jonathan Edwards, 25, Sermons and Discourses, 1743–1758*, edited
by Wilson H. Kimnach (New Haven: Yale University Press, 2006), 82–102.

hand, a truly divine and holy heat and ardor is ever accompanied
with light.

That both heat and light may be acquired by the aspiring preacher,
Edwards urges him to be "diligent in [his] studies," "very conversant
with the holy Scriptures," and "much in seeking God, and conversing
with him by prayer, who is the fountain of light and love." All in all,
Edwards' ideal does not seem to be very different from that of the tradi-
tional preacher of the time, except that in the full context of the sermon
and through the extensive use of light imagery, he suggests a standard
of transcendent dedication and nearly mystical fervor that is rare in any
age. And like Stoddard before him, Edwards cultivated a subtle personal
tone in his rhetoric that, more than any stated principle, demonstrates
the risk-taking commitment demanded of the good preacher.

Edwards is best known for his defenses of passionate emotion,
including "hellfire," in revival preaching. And, indeed, in *Religious
Affections* he argues that "such means are to be desired, as have much of
a tendency to move the affections."[8] Moreover, in *Some Thoughts on the
Revival of Religion in New England*, he emphatically insists that

> Though . . . clearness of distinction and illustration, and strength
> of reason, and a good method, in the doctrinal handling of the
> truths of religion, is many ways needful and profitable, and not
> to be neglected. . . . Our people don't so much need to have their
> heads stored, as to have their hearts touched; and they stand in
> the greatest need of that sort of preaching that has the greatest
> tendency to do this.[9]

As for "hellfire" preaching in particular, Edwards argues:

> Some talk of it as an unreasonable thing to think to fright per-
> sons to heaven; but I think it is a reasonable thing to endeavor to
> fright persons away from hell . . . 'tis a reasonable thing to fright
> a person out of an house on fire.

As for the style or manner of "hellfire" preaching, he makes this observation:

> When ministers preach of hell, and warn sinners to avoid it, in
> a cold manner, though they may say in words that it is infinitely

8. *The Works of Jonathan Edwards, 2, Religious Affections*, edited by John E. Smith
(New Haven: Yale University Press, 1959), 121.

9. *The Works of Jonathan Edwards, 4, Great Awakening*, edited by C. C. Goen (New
Haven: Yale University Press, 1972), 387–88.

terrible; yet (if we look on language as a communication of our minds to others) they contradict themselves; for actions, as I observed before, have a language to convey our minds, as well as words; and at the same time that such a preacher's words represents the sinner's state as infinitely dreadful, his behavior and manner of speaking contradict it, and show that the preacher don't think so; so that he defeats his own purpose; for the language of his actions, in such a case, is much more effectual than the bare signification of his words.[10]

Edwards might well have extended this comment to include the "gesture of language"—specifically, images and metaphors employed in making an argument concrete—in the case of printed sermons.

In summary, it should be observed that, while Edwards placed no limits on the intensity of emotion that a preacher might attempt to evoke through his preaching, he insisted upon a constant balance and aesthetically pleasing harmony between emotion and thought. Indeed, he insisted that without a duly precise and comprehensive body of theological concepts in the sermon, there is no religion at all.[11]

Edwards' ideal preacher is, then, a figure of commanding intellectual rigor and overwhelming rhetorical power; he strikes a blow for religion simultaneously in the heads and hearts of his auditors, though with an emphasis upon the heart. In the performance of his duty, he shows that he is the peculiarly designated servant of his Master:

They should imitate [Christ] in the manner of his preaching; who taught not as the Scribes, but with authority, boldly, zealously and fervently; insisting chiefly on the most important things in religion, being much in warning men of the danger of damnation, setting forth the greatness of the future misery of the ungodly; insisting not only on the outward, but also the inward and spiritual duties of religion: being much in declaring the great provocation and danger of spiritual pride, and a self-righteous disposition; yet much insisting on the necessity and importance of inherent holiness, and the practice of piety . . . wonderfully adapting his discourse to persons, seasons and occasions.[12]

10. WJE 4:247–48.

11. For an extended discussion of JE's ideas on the necessity of intellectual substance in sermons, see his sermon, *The Importance and Advantage of a Thorough Knowledge of Divine Truth*, in WJE 22:80–102.

12. *Christ the Example of Ministers*, WJE 25:339.

If a congregation could "hear and stand it out" under such preaching, there would probably be little hope for the English language as an instrument of salvation.

### The Sermon in Edwards' Hands

The development and ultimate deterioration of the sermon form in Edwards' hands will be discussed shortly, but now an attempt must be made to define the formal limits of the Edwardsean sermon at the zenith of its development during the late 1720s, the 1730s, and the very early 1740s (and whenever Edwards had an important preaching occasion in subsequent years and returned to that form and style).[13] This sermon is a formal literary unit consisting of three main divisions, Text, Doctrine, and Application. There is only one significant variation in the form, which is called a "lecture." The lecture is differentiated from the sermon only through the altered proportions in the Doctrine and Application. For whereas in the sermon the Application is usually a little longer than the Doctrine and often several times as long, in the lecture the Doctrine is substantially longer than the Application. Perhaps the best-known instance of the lecture variant is *A Divine and Supernatural Light* (1734), which has a doctrine of twenty-three pages, and an Application of a little over three pages in the first edition.

Otherwise, so far as *form* is concerned, a sermon is a sermon—whether pastoral, imprecatory, occasional, doctrinal, or whatever.[14] Of course, this does not mean that the form was ever so fixed as to restrict variations; indeed, there were always so many variations that the very identity of the sermon as a literary form seems at times threatened. If the variations possible within the three main divisions are considered, however, it is evident that Edwards never lost sight of the paradigm.

13. The recovery in the early 1980s of JE's original MS of the *Farewell Sermon* (1750) provided confirmation that, though he employed scrap paper in all late sermons, JE returned to writing out all sermons he considered important.

14. Sermons based upon Old Testament texts tend to have longer Doctrines than those based upon New Testament texts, resulting in some lessening of emphasis upon Application in Old Testament-text sermons. This phenomenon seems to result from a necessity for relating Old Testament materials to the gospel message, which is effected in the Doctrine.

## Text

The Text begins the sermon, invariably with the Scripture passage upon which the formal structure of the sermon rests. Indeed, it is the verse citation of the initial Scripture passage, rather than a word or phrase from the doctrine, that identifies a sermon when it is referred to in Edwards' notebooks. There is no exordium or introduction before the reading of the Scripture text, and there need not be any explication or exegesis after it, if the meaning is obvious, in order to have a complete Text. In the vast majority of sermons, however, there is a brief passage (a page, more or less) of comment and explication following the scriptural passage which Edwards designates the Opening of the Text. The Opening consists of several brief, numbered heads, frequently designated "Observation" or "Inference," in which Edwards defines difficult terms, cites other Scripture passages that parallel or complement the textual passage, and generally explains its meaning. In explication, he is never pedantic, even on those rare occasions when he introduces Hebrew or Greek words to clarify definitions; he explains carefully, but does not belabor small points. Indeed, some students of Edwards have felt the Opening of the Text to be the finest part of the sermon because of Edwards' remarkable ability to narrate the statements and events of the text as immediate experience, and in his narrations he not infrequently displays the talent of a first-rate journalist or novelist. But his narrations present concise sketches rather than murals, and the Text is never long.

## Doctrine

Following the Text is the Doctrine, a major portion of most sermons and, structurally, often the most complex. The Doctrine usually begins with a single statement of doctrine, carefully labeled "Doc[trine]." In his inclination to formulate the entire doctrinal message of the sermon in a single statement of doctrine, Edwards was, it seems, a little unusual for his day. Most contemporary preachers tended to formulate two or more equally important statements and list them in parallel at the head of the Doctrine. Although it is Edwards' custom to draw two, three, or four Propositions or Observations from the doctrine immediately after its statement, thus dividing it for "clearing" or full discussion in the body of the Doctrine, the single statement of doctrine brings the entire sermon into a sharp thematic focus, like light rays passing through a lens, if only for a vivid moment.

But there need be no formal statement of doctrine at all. Sometimes, when the Scripture text is a clear, concise statement of thesis in itself and in need of no explication, Text and Doctrine elide and the Scripture quotation becomes the statement of doctrine, or, as Edwards puts it, the doctrine is "supplied." At other times, though rarely in Edwards' best days of preaching, there is no statement labeled "Doc[trine]," but only one or two propositions.[15] In such cases, the Proposition differs not at all from the usual statement of doctrine, unless it be a little less assertive in tone.

After the statement of doctrine and the division of the statement into Propositions, Edwards takes up the propositions, explaining the import of each and developing its implications through Inquiries, Observations, Arguments, and plain numbered heads. Each Proposition is also "proved" through Reasons. The term "reason" is actually a generic term for all "proofs" under the Doctrine, and Edwards does not frequently use it as the name for a particular head. The proofs of the doctrine are of two basic types: citations of Scripture (often attended with interpretation), and appeals to human reason and commonplace experience.

Most of the time, particularly in the shorter and middle-length sermons, the Doctrine ends with the giving of various reasons or proofs. However, each Proposition may have its own Use, Improvement, or Application, especially in the longer sermons. This occurs most often when the various propositions have quite different practical implications, and Edwards feels compelled to spell out the different duties implied by each Proposition. However, these uses are within the division of the Doctrine and are not to be confused with the third main division of the sermon. In sermons where such "doctrinal uses" are employed, Edwards often differentiates them from the third main division by calling it the "Application of the Whole."

---

15. A hallmark of the Stockbridge Indian sermons is that, whether written out or in bare outline, they have nothing labeled "Doc[trine]," but only Propositions or Observations, despite being virtual synopses of earlier sermons which had formal statements of doctrine.

*Application*

The Application (or Improvement or Use) is the largest of the three main divisions of the sermon (except in the lecture variant), and in long sermons it may be several times as long as the Text and Doctrine together. It is usually marked by a significant alteration in tone and rhetoric, and by a comparatively simple structure; for whereas the Text and Doctrine are concerned with theory, principle, and precept, the Application is concerned with experience and practice. The Application is directed to specific thoughts, attitudes, and actions of living human beings, and it gives specific advice on these attitudes and actions, in poignant language, in the light of the sermon's doctrine. But as employed by Edwards, the Application also has a subtler use as is indicated by his own statement in this transitional passage between the Doctrine and Application of Genesis 19:14.

> The Improvement we shall make of this doctrine shall be to offer some considerations to make future punishment seem real to you.

In effect, then, the Application is a period of hypothetical experience for Edwards' auditory, a time of living imaginatively, through a "willing suspension of disbelief," a series of fictive experiences created and controlled by the preacher.

*Uses*

The Application or Improvement is generally structured by division into several Uses. Most of the time, the term "use" is restricted to serving as the categorical name for main heads under the division of "Application" or "Improvement," paralleling "reasons" in the Doctrine. (The two division names, incidentally, are used interchangeably, though "Application" appears to be the favored term after the first few years of preaching.) Thus, there is frequently a Use of Self-examination, or a Use of Consolation, and up to four or five such "specialized" uses, though the concluding use is most often the Use of Exhortation. Each Use is subdivided by Inquiries, Considerations, and plain numbered heads, and a list of Considerations or Directions generally concludes the Use of Exhortation.

There are several "paired" heads, such as Objection-Consideration, Enquiry-Answer, and Positive-Negative, that may appear under any one of the three major divisions of the sermon as they are needed, as may such heads as Inference, Observation, or Inquiry. In fact, it should be noted that the minor heads are generally employed in a very flexible way, and are inserted wherever they fit. Few are used only in the Text, Doctrine, or the Application.

In order to have a complete Edwardsean sermon, then, there must be an identifying passage of Scripture at the beginning and an Application (of the whole) at the end; in the middle, there must be a doctrinal discussion of the Bible text, though not necessarily an Opening of the Text or an explicitly labeled "Doc[trine]." The minimal requirements are comparatively easy to describe; the difficulties arise when one attempts to define the "outer limits" of the sermon form.

First, there is the problem of literary form versus pulpit performance. Edwards sometimes speaks of a single preaching session in the pulpit, and that portion of a long sermon that might be preached in one session, as "a sermon"; but he also speaks of a complex literary unit, which includes several clearly marked preaching units within it, as "a sermon." Apparently he was not alone in his ambiguity, for in several eighteenth-century editions his longer sermons are printed as a series of sermons (according to preaching units) rather than as the single long sermons that, according to the form, they are. Such printing conventions preserve the root sense of the Latin *sermo* which means "talk"; moreover, they preserve the spirit of the seventeenth-century New England sermon as a speech act only incidentally preserved in print. When editing his own sermons for the press, however, Edwards scrupulously called sermons of more than one preaching unit "discourses," as in *Discourses on Various Important Subjects*, where some pieces are of one preaching unit and others of more. Modern readers especially must treat the Text-Doctrine-Application unit—however long—as a literary unit: otherwise, they will probably miss theme, logic, and form altogether.

Even when one admits that a sermon may be of any length, as long as it is carefully constructed, without losing its formal unity, there is the complication created by the "paired sermons" and the sermon series. In the case of the paired sermons, Edwards may write two sermons on the same text to be preached in series; however, they share nothing, not even the Opening of the Text, beyond the initial Scripture text. Obviously they are two sermons, though they may, if they are brief, be delivered on the same day. Then there is the variant in which Edwards announces two doctrines in two sermons, but develops only the first doctrine in the first sermon and only the second doctrine in the second sermon. Again, though the sermons are obviously meant to go together, they are formally separated. Such variations, when multiplied, led to the several sermon series which Edwards wrote and preached in the 1730s, including the one presented here.

Obviously, somewhere between the morning-and-afternoon sermon, divided between the Doctrine and the Application so that it could fill the entire Sabbath-day services, and the over-two-hundred-page, thirty-preaching-unit sermon series, the form of the sermon begins to disintegrate. Edwards became a master of his inherited sermon form, but in the 1730s, at the zenith of his mastery, he began experimenting artistically with the sermon. He apparently did everything he could do without actually abandoning the old form entirely, and the only possible conclusion one can draw from the manuscript evidence of his experiments is that he was searching, consciously or unconsciously, for a formal alternative to the sermon itself.

# INTRODUCTION
## The Historical Context

Kenneth P. Minkema and Adriaan C. Neele

JONATHAN EDWARDS DELIVERED HIS SERMON SERIES ON THE PARABLE of the Net, as found in Matthew 13, in at least eleven, and probably twelve, installments from May to July 1746. Compared to other significant series on Matthean parables, such as that on the wise and foolish virgins and on the sower,[1] which were preached between or just on the cusp of awakenings, *Fish Out of Their Element* is post-awakening, and so is retrospective. From Christ's parable, Edwards draws twelve observations concerning false and true Christians, and how to discriminate between them—a topic that takes up other major series on the Matthean parables, such as that of the wise and foolish virgins.

### WAR AND REBELLION

It is important to have some acquaintance with the historical events of that time, because they place in dramatic context Edwards' activities as a commentator on what he saw as the nature of true religion through treatises and sermons. He preached this series amidst tumultuous circumstances, of local and transatlantic import. Since 1744, nearly all of Europe had been engulfed in the War of Austrian Succession, known in the American theater as King George's War. The great French fortress at

---

1. For these series, see *Sermons by Jonathan Edwards on the Matthean Parables, Volume I: True and False Christians (On the Parable of the Wise and Foolish Virgins),* and *Volume II: Divine Husbandmen (On the Parable of the Sower and the Seed)* (Eugene, OR: Cascade, 2012).

Louisburg in Canada had unexpectedly fallen in 1745 to English colonial forces, but conflict with the French and their Indian allies continued. In the spring of 1746, native bands raided English settlements from New Hampshire to New York. In May, watchtowers were built around Northampton to detect approaching enemy parties, and Edwards' home was "forted in" and quartered with soldiers against attacks. Meanwhile, Massachusetts Governor William Shirley had received permission to mount a new attack on Quebec, which was to be a joint expedition of British and American forces.[2] Colonial governments and militia prepared for the new campaign and by June, as the people of Northampton listened to Edwards expound on the parable of the net—and, presumably, read their pastor's latest work on *Religious Affections*—they were ready to march. Indeed, Edwards interrupted his discourse on the parable of the net to preach a militia sermon in June "preceding the expedition to Canada" (no. 824), and, at the series' conclusion, for the July fast "on occasion of the expedition to Canada" (no. 832).

In that same eventful spring, word reached the colonies that the second Jacobite rebellion—"The Forty-Five"—had begun when Prince Charles Stuart, "the Young Pretender," sailed from France to Scotland in the summer of 1745 to revive his father's cause of three decades earlier to re-establish the Stuart dynasty. (Edwards preached a fast sermon "occasioned by the rebellion" on March 13 [no. 812].) With vague promises of French assistance, the Prince raised a small army from among the clans, enjoyed some initial success against English forces (who were otherwise engaged on the continent), and by the end of the year had come within 120 miles of London. During the winter, however, the rebel army turned north and was heading toward its denouement in the spring of 1746, at the battle of Culloden. It was not until August that the provinces learned of the defeat of the Prince and his forces.[3]

It was in this context, fraught with immediate danger threatening political upheaval and religious persecution that made the local contentions of the Great Awakening seem pale by comparison, that Edwards not only published *Religious Affections* but preached on the parable of the net. Both of these efforts took on the air of martial protestant statements

2. On King George's War, see Howard H. Peckham, *The Colonial Wars, 1689–1762* (Chicago: University of Chicago Press, 1964), 97–120.

3. On the Jacobite Rebellion, see Diana Preston, *The Road to Culloden Moor: Bonnie Prince Charlie and the '45 Rebellion* (London: Constable, 1995).

against threats of Catholic incursions in Scotland and in North America. The sermonic effort complements, supports, and extends the treatise, and stands on its own as an important statement on the nature of the church, sainthood, and divine judgment.

The series also interacts with sermons that preceded and followed it. Edwards used Joshua 24:15 as his text twice within the space of three months, first at the February quarterly lecture, where he discussed religion and good order in families (no. 807); and secondly in April, to encourage diffident or lukewarm believers to come "to some full and positive determination with themselves" to do what God requires (no. 815). In February, he had also encouraged prayer for the "great outpouring of the Spirit that God has promised in the latter days" (no. 809). What is especially prominent in the weeks just before he commences *Fish Out of Their Element*, and interspersed with the actual preaching of his consideration of the parable of the net, is the frequency with which he considers trinitarian and related themes: on the union of Christ and believers (no. 810); on God the Father (no. 813); on the Son (no. 818); and on the Holy Spirit (no. 819).

## THEMES IN THE DISCOURSE

Jesus' homely, workaday image of fishing provides the starting point for this discourse. Fishermen catch fish indiscriminately in a net, then separate the good from the bad. From this basic trope, Edwards constructs his series of "Observations." The conversion of sinners may fitly be compared to taking fish in a net, he begins, because natural men, like fish, are "in their element, wild and ungoverned," and because they are taken against their will. God, the author of conversion, is the one wielding the power, who encloses sinners on every side with his net and seizes them by convictions "in the depths of security." These points instruct natural men of their sinful condition, which they cannot change by themselves, that the awakening of some sinners does not result in conversion, much like the catching in some fish in a net does not result in their being kept. From this, we learn what will happen to those that God does not enclose in his net, and so how great a thing it is to be converted.

God's mercy and grace extend to all sorts of persons, the second Observation tells us. With no doctrinal development, Edwards goes right to Application, asserting that God calls on all sorts of persons to forsake sin and seek salvation: old aged, middle-aged, children, those low and poor, those "weak in understanding," those that are despised, those in "higher circumstances," those living in immorality and backsliding, those who have long sought God's grace, and "dark and melancholic persons."

Many seem to be converted, Edwards allows, but not as many as we would be lead to believe. False converts—those who think and claim they are converted—may seem to be converted if we are to judge by external and internal "resemblances" with true converts. External similarities include profession, "show," performance of duties—all, to Edwards' estimation, pharisaical, for personal aggrandizement—and especially frequent during times of the outpouring of God's Spirit. Internal similarities include the number and variety of seeming graces and experiences, and their similarity in kind or type; also, the production of counterfeit grace may seem to be the same as true grace. Because of these close affinities, believers must take care that they are not deceived, and beware of things that increase their liability to be deceived (though Edwards does not explain here what those "things" are). Knowing how easily individuals can become set in an opinion of themselves as true converts, and how difficult it is to be brought off from it, Edwards recommends constant self-scrutiny, a sort of spiritual flexibleness. Offering a string of advice, he exhorts his hearers not to rest in an appearance of grace, not to depend on others' judgment, or on anything that is not beyond the experience of natural men. Do not be content with a "first work," or an initial presumed conversion experience, but only in a habitual, enlightened sense that increases awakenings and convictions, a sense of need, and an appetite for seeking God.

Observation IV states that, just as the netted fish, wicked men cannot always enjoy their "element," but sooner or later must be separated from it. Some natural men are brought out of their state by conversion, but if not so, then by death, and never to return. Take heed, Edwards directs, that this is not your fate. Consider the properties and circumstances of the sorrow and rage of hell, which is perfect, without mitigation, and yields nothing but further sorrow and rage. Likewise, asserts the next Observation, the wicked shall not always be mixed with the righteous, as in the net of fish, or in the visible church.

But the wicked and the righteous will be separated at the last day of the world, which "must come to an end." This will not be, as some contemporaries of Edwards asserted, by annihilation, or a complete obliteration of all the world. Not all of the inhabitants shall cease to be, but the "frame" of the world will be destroyed, and with it will come a total and eternal end of the present state of humankind. This apocalyptic note leads Edwards to exhort believers to improve their time in this world, to make sure of their redemption from it; here, there is still an opportunity for salvation. Be engrafted into the stock of Christ, build your hope on Christ the Rock, forsake the world, and improve your life in this world as a journey to the eternal realm.

Apocalyptic urgency resounds in the next Observation, where Edwards asserts that once the "full number" of the elect is gathered in, the end of the world will soon come. There is a certain number God has chosen from eternity, and they must all be gathered to God before the close of all things earthly. Several things "secure" this order of events, including the greatness of God's love to them, God's promise to his Son, God's immutability, the great price paid by Christ, Christ's concern for his honor, the incompleteness of Christ mystical without the church, the sufficiency of Christ, and Christ's "proper capacity" to gather them through his intercession. With the elect secured, the world will be destroyed as promised in Scripture and necessitated by God's wrath against wickedness. For now, it is only the presence of God's church that prevents the world from falling further into darkness. This lower world, too, is a stage for the work of redemption, which must be carried to completion. These points demonstrate the value God sets on the elect and the importance of making their election sure. The saints need to behave themselves "as becomes those that stand in the gap."

God will treat the elect as his special portion, his prize. They are his portion by relation, nearness and interest, chosen apart for special use, that part of humankind to which God takes delight in communicating himself and in which he takes delight in beholding. God will treat the elect as his prize, not because he depends on them but because of his sovereign pleasure. None shall be lost, and they shall be out of harm's way. In heaven, God will "solace himself" in them. On the other hand, God will "cast away unsound professors," those who present themselves as elect but who are false. God will "discover" (i.e., reveal) them, show he has no value for them, no more improve them, and finally remove them from his presence. How agonizing, Edwards proclaims, will it be for such to see true saints admitted into heaven while they are cast away. To prevent such a tragedy, do not despise divine things, do not separate yourself from God, do not reject the Spirit of God—don't cast yourself away—but improve the day of God's mercy and be upright in profession and duties.

Edwards then spends an entire preaching unit on angels. Why? Angels, of course, are mentioned in the text. Nonetheless, angels, as he points out, cannot find out a way of salvation, cannot purchase salvation, cannot convert or carry on the work of sanctification, cannot act as judges, and are not the authors of glorification or damnation. But they are vital as "ministers" in the affairs relating to the eternal state of humankind. They give means of grace through revelations and assistance, they were ministering spirits to Christ while on earth, they continue to minister in resisting evil angels, they conduct the souls of the holy to heaven at death, they will help to separate the wicked on the day of judgment, and execute vengeance on the ungodly. Saints, therefore, should seek the privilege of the ministration of angels. Avoid the sins upon which angels will execute God's wrath, such as lust, obstinacy, and self-exaltation. Seek an interest in Christ, the head of the angels, strive to be like the angels, and be found in the way to heaven.

For nearly all of the remainder of the series, Edwards considers the fate of the damned. When angels aid in segregating the wicked on the day of judgment, the place to which the wicked shall be conducted is "a furnace of fire." (In his "Miscellanies," Edwards describes this furnace as the contents of the universe that will implode in a massive conflagration—the mirror opposite of the Big Bang.)[4] God's wrath in Scripture is compared to fire, because God burns against sin; there is in that fire "a great manifestation of God's strength." The damned will be tossed, against their wills and in total misery, into the extreme heat of an infinite state of torment. All the fires that men and God have "kindled" in this world are but types or foreshadows of the fires of hell. The misery of the damned will be perfect, a mixture of sorrow and rage: sorrow in consideration of things past, present, and future; rage against their companions, against God, against the saints, and against themselves. The concluding Use, by contrast, describes how different the state of the saints in glory shall be. To achieve this blessed condition, Edwards provides a round of directions: mortify hellish principles, come to Christ who has suf-

---

4. See, for example, "Miscellanies" no. 931, in *Works of Jonathan Edwards, 20, "Miscellanies" 833–1152*, edited by Amy Plantinga Pauw (New Haven: Yale University Press, 2002), 187.

fered, avoid anything that will bring regret hereafter and seek instead godly sorrow and well-founded religious joys. Comply with "the bitter and hard things" that religion requires, and get your heart "calmed and sweetened with those principles that are contrary to rage."

## THE DISCOURSE ON THE NET
## AND RELIGIOUS AFFECTIONS

The delivery of this sermon paralleled the publication of *Religious Affections* in June 1746, and the sermon discovers the same intricate searching of religious experience as the treatise. There are several close parallels between sermon and treatise, particularly in regard to Observation III. The First Positive Sign of *Religious Affections* has the same the discussion of the "resemblances" between the "internal exercises of hypocrites and true converts," and of the description of "imaginary ideas." Also, the similarity of unconverted and converted in "external appearance" through profession, "show," and performance of duties parallels the Third Negative Sign. And the discussion of depending upon a "first work" relates to the Eleventh Positive Sign. Otherwise, the Applications of this sermon series extend the arguments of *Religious Affections* into areas that the treatise only mentions in passing, if at all, including the role of angels as ministering spirits, the end of the world, the nature of hell, and the misery of the damned.

Finally, Edwards re-cast this sermon series for the Indians at Stockbridge in January 1751.[5] In a single sermon, he condenses and adapts the earlier, larger discourse, this time focusing on the fisherman as the pastor, with the Doctrine, "The fishermen that cast the net are ministers of the gospel whom Christ appoints to gather men into his church." Good and bad are still mixed together in the church on earth, but at the day of judgment all will be sorted out. As the new minister at the Indian mission, Edwards explained, his role was to "gather" in the elect souls among his new charges.

---

5. Printed as *Heaven's Dragnet* in WJE 25:575–81.

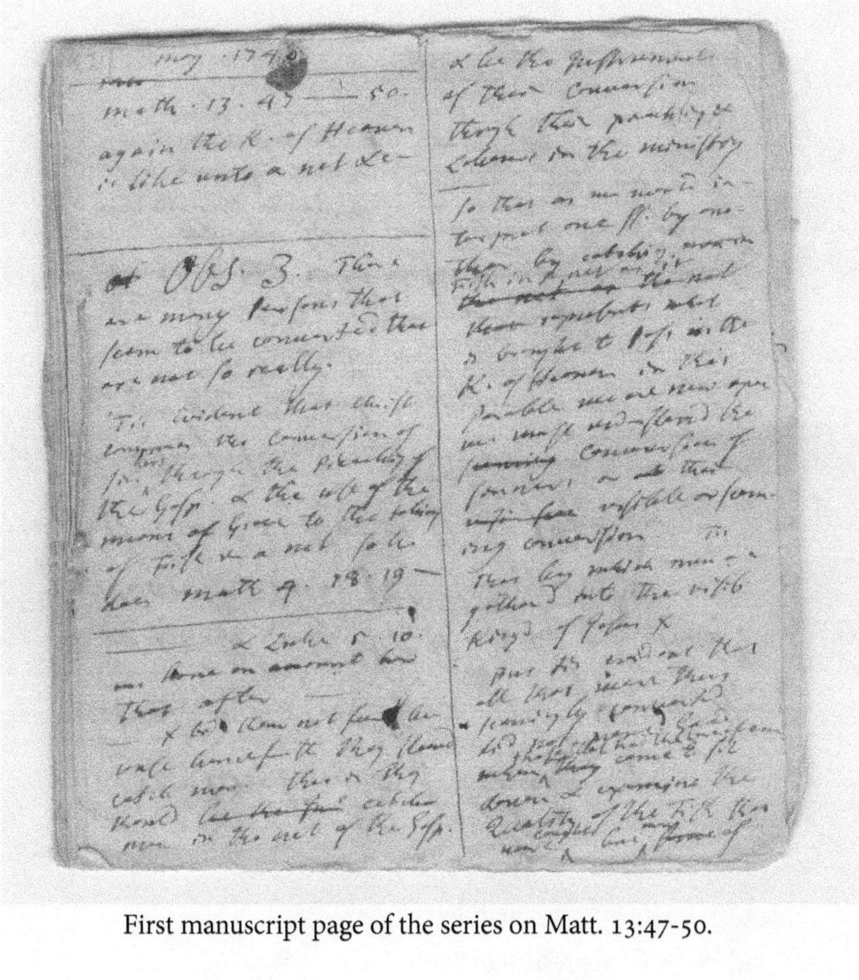

First manuscript page of the series on Matt. 13:47-50.

# FISH OUT THEIR ELEMENT
## (The Parable of the Net)

Matthew 13:47–50.

*Again, the kingdom of heaven is like unto a net, that was cast into the sea, and gathered of every kind: which, when it was full, they drew to shore, and sat down, and gathered the good unto the vessels, but cast the bad away. So shall it be at the end of the world: the angels shall come forth, and sever the wicked from among the just, and shall cast them into the furnace of fire: there shall be wailing and gnashing of teeth.*

THE PASSAGE OF SCRIPTURE THAT HAS BEEN READ CONSISTS OF TWO parts, viz., a parable, and its explanation. In the former we have,

　　1. The thing represented: the kingdom of heaven.

　　2. The similitude.

In the explanation is explained who are represented by the fish that are taken, viz.,

[1.] Who [are represented] by the good.

[2.] [Who are represented] by the bad.

[3.] [Who are represented] by those that sever the fish one from another: angels.

[4.] What time there is respect to in the parable, in those words, "when it was full, they drew to shore, and sat down, and gathered the good into vessels, but cast the bad away": [the] end of the world.

[5.] What is implied in the bad being cast away.

[6.] And lastly, the consequence of this is declared: "There shall be wailing."

From the words that have been read, several observations may be raised.

## OBSERVATION I.

*The conversion of sinners may fitly be compared to the taking fish in a net.*

And that, on the following account:

*First.* Men in their natural state are like fish at liberty in their element, wild and ungoverned.

Natural men in their sins, and in the enjoyment and pursuit of their lusts, their worldly pleasures, profits and honors, and in their evil practice, are in their element. The nature of man, as he is by nature, is sinful, and wickedness is as natural to him—that which he is, is naturally inclined to and delights [in], and what he naturally lives in and lives by—as water is to a fish.

As a fish constantly lives in the water, {so natural men constantly live in their sins}.

As a fish, contrary to the nature of all other animals, lives without breath, so [natural men live] without the influences of the Spirit of God.

The air, which is the very life of other animals, is what is exceeding contrary to the nature {of a fish}; so {the Spirit of God is contrary to natural men}.

The nature of man, as he is by nature, is as diverse from that of the children of God, as {the nature of fish is from other animals}: that which one lives by, is the death of the other.

That which drowns and quickly kills other animals, is the life of fishes, and their delight; so [natural men delight in their sin].

Fishes at their liberty in the sea, are wild and out of the possession and government of mankind; so natural men are far off from God, are not subject to the law of God, will not be controlled by God's commands and held within the limits of their duty to him, being aliens and strangers, and under the power of a carnal mind that is not subject to the law of God, neither indeed can be.

Man is born as the wild ass' colt, Job 11:12, that is noted as an animal that is not [to] be subject to the government of mankind, that cannot be tamed, or kept to rules, or held under restraints by human discipline. See Job 39:5–8, "Who hath sent out the wild ass free? or who hath loosed the bands of the wild ass? Whose house I have made the wilderness, and the barren land his dwellings. He scorneth the multitude of the city, neither regardeth he the crying of the driver. The range of the mountains is his pasture, and he searcheth after every green thing." Jer. 2:24, "A wild ass used to the wilderness, that snuffeth up the wind at her pleasure; in her occasion who can turn her away?"

*Second.* The conversion of sinners may fitly be compared to the taking of fish in a net, inasmuch as it is not of themselves, but is wholly the effect of the power, will and design of another.

The fishes being taken in a net, is an effect that is not of them. 'Tis nothing agreeable to their inclination, no fruit of their design or contrivance, but contrary to their will.

So is the conversion of a sinner. Sinners, if left to themselves, would choose to continue in their sins. And thus it is with sinners, even to the very time of their conversions. Although there are many sinners that are not yet converted that are awakened, and in some measure sensible of their misery, and are seeking deliverance from their misery, yet {they continue in their sins}.

Conversion is really not the thing that they aim at. [They] are enemies to conversion. They are not properly designing any such thing; are striving against it; and their hearts do wholly oppose it, till the moment that they are actually converted.

[Conversion is] not the effect of their power or strength, not the effect of their contrivance, not the consequence of the natural tendency of anything they do, not agreeable to their wills. 'Tis from God, as counteracting their natures and their inclinations, aims and designs, as much as the taking of a fish in a net is not from the fish, but the fisherman, altogether the fruit of the will, power, design and contrivance of the fisherman.

If the fish were left to himself, he never would be taken {in a net}; so [with the natural man].

*Third.* The conversion of sinners is the fruit of the peculiar wisdom and skill of the Author if it, and also secondarily of the instrument of it.

As the taking fish in a net is owing to the fisherman's art[1]—men are wont to exercise their cunning and display their art in catching of birds and fishes and other animals that are wild—so the bringing souls out of a state of nature home to the Lord Jesus Christ is an effect of the wonderful wisdom of God. This is the wisdom spoken of, Prov. 8:12, "[I] dwell with prudence, and find out knowledge of witty inventions."

The wisdom of God wonderfully appears in what he has done, whereby a foundation is laid for the conversion and salvation of sinners. Eph. 1:8, "abounded in all wisdom and prudence." Eph. 3:10,[2] "the manifold wisdom of God."

And the wisdom of God commonly wonderfully appears in preparing the way for, and bringing about the effect itself, of a sinner's conversion: [in] disposals of providence; turning the temptations, subtil devices and violent assaults of Satan against himself; overruling the exercises of the corruption {of nature}; conducting the soul through the terrible [snares]; [and] leading it along in a marvelous manner through the mazes and labyrinths it is brought into.

So then it is commonly so, when a sinner is converted and comforted, and comes to look back, those dealings of God with him that appeared most mysterious and dark in the time of it, now appear plain.

And so is God pleased to make use of means in this affair, that the conversion of sinners is commonly secondarily owing to the wisdom and skill of ministers of the gospel, that are called fishermen; and those of them that are faithful, have a holy skill, and a kind of divine art given to them by their Lord and Master, who has made them fishers of men. He instructs them in the art of catching men. Some of them, he makes wise as serpents; makes [them] wise scribes; gives 'em the tongue of the learned. This holy skill the apostle Paul used, and was abundantly successful in it.

*Fourth.* The sinner, before his actual conversion, is as it were enclosed round on every side by God's net, as the fish is first enclosed by the net of the fisherman before he is drawn out of the water. Hos. 2:6–7, "Therefore, behold, I will hedge up thy way with thorns, and make a

---

1. This phrase evokes the first and most popular description of "the art of angling," Izaak Walton's *The compleat angler or, The contemplative man's recreation. Being a discourse of fish and fishing, not unworthy the perusal of most anglers, a popular fishing manual of the time* (London, 1653).

2. MS: "Eph. 2. 10."

wall, that she shall not find her paths. And she shall follow after her lovers, but she shall not overtake them; and she shall seek them, but shall not find them: then shall she say, I will go and return to my first husband; for then was it better with me than now." [The sinner is] pent up more and more closely, [has] less and less room.

*Fifth.* Sinners are often seized by convictions in order to their[3] conversion, when just before they were in the depths of security.

[When] in the midst of their career in sins.

[Such as the] apostle Paul.

*Sixth.* Sinners are commonly brought home to Christ in a way very unexpected to them. [They] are laying out ways, [they] form motives; but [they] are all wrong, [they] can have no idea.

When [they] think themselves nearest, [they] are furthest off. When [they] think themselves furthest off, [they] are nearest.

[It occurs by] unexpected means, and in an unexpected way; the event is quite unexpected.

All [is] new and strange.

Ps. 126:1, "we were like them that dream."

*Seventh.* The drawing of [fish] out of the water by the [net], is death to 'em. So the conversion of sinners is often spoken of in Scripture as being in several respects the death of the sinner.

*Eighth.* Sinners are oftentimes converted in great numbers at a time.

## APPLICATION.

I. What has been observed may be of conviction unto those that are in a natural condition, to convince them of their sin and misery, and how justly they might be left to perish.

[You are] like fish in your element.

[You live] constantly [in your sins].

Your life [is wild and ungoverned].

[You have a] nature exceeding contrary [to God].

[You] are enemies to your own life.

[You are] ungoverned and untamable.

You continually oppose your own conversion and salvation.

[This] shows your misery.

[This] shows how just [God would be to condemn you].

3. MS: "the."

II. And from what has been observed, we may learn the reason why the awakenings of some sinners do not issue in their conversion, viz., because they don't find themselves on every side enclosed in God's net.

[The fish] yet has room in the water.

Many are like fish partly enclosed, and are affrighted, but make their escape through a gap. Is. 57:10, "Thou art wearied in the greatness of the way."

III. From what has been observed, we may learn what will become of those that God lets alone, and don't seize them by his irresistible and efficacious power and grace.

They will be caught in a net indeed, in another sense.

IV. From what has been observed, we may learn how great a thing it is to be indeed converted

['Tis a] changing their element.

['Tis a] changing their very nature as much.

'Tis death.

['Tis] without any assistance or concurrence from sinners,[4] but against an universal opposition.

V. Hence, let all sinners that are concerned for their salvation be warned not to trust in themselves, as though their conversion was ever likely to be owing to their own power, will or wisdom.

Thus sinners are wont to do.

[They] imagine that [they can convert themselves].

[This is] owing to their great ignorance.

Ignorance of two things especially:

[*First.*] Ignorance of themselves.

Their own insufficiency.

Ignorance of their hearts, {of} their aims.

[*Second.*] Ignorance of the nature of conversion, not knowing what manner of thing it is.

But what has been observed shows the vanity {of trusting in ourselves}.

Their trusting is one instance of their opposing [God].

VI. From what has been observed, we may learn what reason they that are converted are under to adore sovereign grace.

'Tis owing to that.[5]

---

4. MS: "sinners that."

5. MS: "them."

If you had been let alone, you would forever have gone on. Yea, if God had not as it were arose and clothed himself with his almighty power, [you would never have been converted].

There was nothing in you tending to it.

All [was] against it.

[You] really acted like fish in a net. [You] strove against [it], continually strove to find the way out.

How froward and perverse was you.

How did the perversement and enmity of your heart appear while God was striving with you.

How wonderful the grace of God in bearing, and how much more wonderfully and finally conquering.[6]

## [DOCTRINE RESUMED.]

[The text is] Matt. 13:47, "and gathered of every kind." Two things seem to be intended:

1. That every kind of persons are brought into the visible kingdom. That this is intended is evident.

2. That persons of all sorts are changed and brought into the spiritual and invisible kingdom of Christ. There is reason to think that this also is intended, because 'tis evident that Christ does often compare conversion, or bringing men out of a state of sin into the spiritual kingdom[7] of Christ, to the taking fish in a net.

## OBSERVATION II.

*The mercy and grace of God revealed in the gospel extends to all sorts of persons.*

## [APPLICATION.]

The *Use* that I would make of this Observation, is to call upon all sorts of persons to forsake their sins, and above all things seek salvation.

[*First.*] Persons of every age.

[1.] Those that are in their youth.

Now you have a most precious opportunity.

---

6. The first preaching unit ends here.
7. MS: "sp. of K."

Indeed, the opportunity that is past is in some respects the best. But that, you have lost. That should stir you up. Consider how much of your life {is spent} already. [The] devil has had your most early days. You have grown up in sin. [As you have] grown in strength and stature, [you have] grown in guilt. You had many calls and warnings when you was a child.

But yet you have a most precious opportunity.

Don't flatter yourself with promises of future opportunity.

[2. I] call upon those that are middle-aged that are in sin, as fish in their element.

How much of your life is gone. Your best season. [It] can't be recovered. You have, it may be, put off in hopes of a better opportunity.

I appeal to you, whether you have found your opportunities grow better. [You] had need to make haste. Most of you are come to have families.

[3. I] come to [those in] old age.

If there be any such that are sensible, [their] case is sorrowful indeed. [You have] spent away first your childhood. What a dreadful load of guilt. What hardness of heart. [In] how many respects have your disadvantages increased. But you are in no less necessity—yea, much greater.

And by what you have heard, you may learn that the mercy {of God} extends [to such as you]. Some are called at the eleventh hour.

Though such as you are the most rarely awakened, yet such above all others have need to be awakened, and to be in good earnest.

And such as you have in many respects more to convince 'em. You have had more experience to convince you. You have had more to convince you of the vanity of the world, more to take off your heart from this world. You have had more to convince you of your own weakness and instability. You have gone through the world, as it were.

[4. To] those that are yet children.

You stand in infinite need {of conversion} as well as others. [You] came into the world in a miserable condition. But yet the mercy {of God} extends to such as you. Yea, you now enjoy the most precious opportunity. Happy are those persons that [improve their opportunity]. Though the opportunity that you enjoy is so good, yet but few improve it.

And this is one reason that there are few saved. Many die in their childhood. Doubtless many children go to hell while they are children. If this should be your case, consider how dreadful your case will be.

Therefore now hearken, lest you at last convince yourself, and say, as Prov. 5:12–13, "How have I hated instruction, and my heart despised reproof; and have not obeyed the voice of my teachers, nor inclined mine ear to them that instructed me."

[*Second.* I] call upon those that [are] comparatively poor and low in the world. [God's grace] extends to such. Many such are called. [You] will not be despised [for] it. The blessed Virgin was poor; Christ was poor. I offer to you this day, in the name of Christ, glorious riches. I Sam. 2:8, "He raiseth the poor [out of the dust, and lifteth up the beggar from the dunghill, to set them amongst princes, and to make them inherit the throne of glory]."

We read of Lazarus [Luke 16:20–25]. Jas. 2:5, "[Hath not God] chosen the [poor of this world rich in faith, and heirs of the kingdom which he promised to them that love him?]"

You have but a little portion in this world; seek a better portion.

You suffer peculiar difficulties and hardships here.

[*Third.* To] those that are weak[8] in understanding.

Mercy extends [to you.]

You are capable of obtaining that wisdom that {is from above}.

[*Fourth.*] You that are despised.

[*Fifth.*] And you that are in higher circumstances in the world than many of your neighbors, hearken. [Mercy extends to] some such as you. [As] "Caesar's household," Philip. 4:22.

Otherwise, all your possessions and outward advantages will be of no advantage. You must in a very little time be stripped {of your possessions}. [You] will be poor. What reasonable comfort can you take in your outward good things, if {you are not saved}? When you sit down at a full table, when you put on better garments, when you take your place above others: these things will all but aggravate your future misery.

Take heed that ben't said to you hereafter, that was said to the rich man when begging for a drop {of water}: "Remember that thou in thy lifetime receivedst thy good things, and likewise Lazarus evil things: but now he is comforted, and thou art tormented" [Luke 16:25]. And take heed you don't do as that other rich man did that we read of, Luke 12:16, etc., "Soul, thou hast much goods [laid up for many years; take thine ease, eat, drink, and be merry. But God said unto him, Thou fool, this

---

8. MS: "are of weak."

night thy soul shall be required of thee: then whose shall those things be, which thou hast provided?]"

[*Sixth.*] Let those that have been great sinners, lived in immoral practices, [hearken]. [Mercy] extends to such as you. We read of many such: I Cor. 9:6, etc.; Col. 2:5, etc.; Tit. 3:3, etc. Indeed your guilt is dreadful {when you sin} under such light. [Your] danger is very great. Especially is this probably the case of some.

[You have] sinned against great opposition of conscience, [in] repeated acts. [You have] been very obstinate. [Your] guilt is grown up to heaven. 'Tis a wonder that God has spared you.

And how dreadful will God's wrath be if {you are not converted}. But yet there is a possibility.

[*Seventh.*] Such as have been guilty of backslidings, [hearken]. Mercy extends to some such. Jer. 3:14, "Turn, O backsliding children, saith the Lord"; [v.] 22, "Return, ye backsliding children, and I will heal your backslidings." Indeed, there is one sort of backsliding {to which mercy does not extend: refusing to return [Jer. 8:5]}. But {yet there is a possibility for such}. There is hope if you can but be persuaded to be in good earnest.

There is the greatest difficulty with backsliders. The judgment of God upon them usually appears in that.

[*Eighth.*] Those that have been long seeking God's grace, and have not yet obtained, [hearken]. Mercy extends [to such]. [As] Saul.

The probable reasons why you have been unsuccessful, [are because you are] not in good earnest, not self-condemned, trusting in yourself, unconvinced of the righteousness of God, blaming God and not yourself.

Thus you have gone on with weapons in your hand, wherewith to fight against God: if now, at length, you can but be persuaded to lay down your weapons.

[*Ninth.*] All dark and melancholic persons, [who are] apt to entertain gloomy apprehensions, to sink in discouragement, have long been in such a way, [hearken].

Grace extends [to such]. God is he that causeth the light to shine out of darkness, gives seeing in the night, and turns the shadow of darkness into the morning. Therefore, lift up the heads that hang down. Don't spend your time and strength in poring on your dark circumstances. Attend to God's voice, consider your duty, apply yourself and persevere in it. If it continues long dark, {continue to seek}. As long as

God continues life, continue to seek him, and cry earnestly to him, and hope and wait for the salvation [of the Lord]. Look to the glorious, all-sufficient, compassionate Redeemer, how far soever you are off, though in the ends of the earth, though in the lions' dens, yea, though as it were in the belly of hell. If you look to him, you will be enlightened. He will strengthen and uphold you with the right hand of his righteousness.

Consider those most encouraging words, Is. 40:27, etc., "Why sayest thou, O Jacob, and speakest, O Israel, My way is hid from the Lord, and my judgment is passed over from my God? Hast thou not known? hast thou not heard, that the everlasting God, the Lord, the Creator of the ends of the earth, fainteth not, neither is weary? there is no searching of his understanding. He giveth power to the faint; and to them that have no might he increaseth strength. Even the youths shall faint and be weary, and the young men shall utterly fall: but they that wait upon the Lord shall renew their strength; they shall mount up with wings as eagles; they shall run, and not be weary; and they shall walk, and not faint."[9]

## [DOCTRINE RESUMED.]
## OBSERVATION III.

*There are many persons that seem to be converted, that are not so really.*

'Tis evident that Christ compares the conversion of sinners through the preaching of the gospel, and the use of the means of grace, to the taking of fish in a net. So he does, Matt. 4:18–19, "And Jesus, walking by the sea of Galilee, saw two brethren, Simon called Peter, and Andrew his brother, casting a net into the sea: for they were fishers. And he saith unto them, Follow me, and I will make you fishers of men." And [in] Luke 5:10, we have an account how that, after {they had taken a great multitude of fishes}, Christ bid them not fear, because henceforth they should catch men; that is, they should catch men in the net of the gospel, and be the instruments of their conversion through their preaching and labors in the ministry.

So that as we would interpret one scripture by another, by catching fish in a net, as it represents what is brought to pass in the kingdom of heaven in this parable we are now upon, we must understand the

---

9. The second preaching unit ends here.

conversion of sinners, or their visible or seeming conversion. 'Tis that by which men are gathered into the visible kingdom of Jesus Christ.

But 'tis evident that all that were thus seemingly converted did not prove good, when those that had the care of 'em came to sit down and examine the quality of the fish that were caught; but many of 'em were good for nothing, and as such were cast away.

So that this observation, that there are many that seem to be converted, {that are not so really}, is justly drawn from the Word.

The same truth is taught us in many other parables of Jesus Christ: [the] sower and the seed [Matt. 13:3–8]; [the] good seed and the tares [Matt. 13:24–30]; the parable of the marriage supper (Matt. 22); [and the] ten virgins [Matt. 25:1–13]. And also in Christ's description of the day of judgment in the 25th of Matthew, latter end.

There are many that are not truly converted that seem to be converted in two respects, viz., by external appearance, and internal resemblance.[10]

*First.* Many have great external appearances of conversion that are not really converted.

There is an external appearance of it in the profession they make. They agree with true converts in the profession of Christianity. [They] profess the same doctrines, profess that God is a being of infinite perfection; that God is worthy; believe a future state; that they are by nature sinners; [and] profess to believe that Christ is sufficient.

Many that are not really converted, make an appearance of being converted, of repentance of soul, and of fearing and loving God above all; and {make a profession and show} in the ordinances they attend, and outward duties of worship they perform, in their prayers to God, in their praises. Many that are not really converted, make a profession and show of conversion and grace in coming to the sacrament of the Lord's Supper; and many that are not truly {converted}, may not only

10. LL. 1–2 of this booklet are made from a discarded marriage bann, which reads:

> This may Certify that the Intention of Marriage
> between Ephraim Wright and Mirriam Wright both
> of Northampton was Entred with <me> on the 11th day of Feb.$^{y}$
> Last. and on 15.th day of S$^{d}$ Month the parties were
> published by Posting Up their Names & Intention
>  In Northampton
> > Attest. Samll Mather Town Clerk
> > Northampton march 26th 1746

attend those duties, but appear very forward and abundant in them, and zealously engaged. Is. 1:12–15, "When ye come to appear before me, who hath required this at your hand, to tread my courts? Bring no more vain oblations; incense is an abomination unto me; the new moons and sabbaths, the calling of assemblies, I cannot away with; it is iniquity, even the solemn meeting. Your new moons and your appointed feasts my soul hateth: they are a trouble unto me; I am weary to hear them. And when ye spread forth your hands, I will hide mine eyes from you: yea, when ye make many prayers, I will not hear: your hands are full of blood." [The] Pharisees fasted twice a week. [Many supposed converts] may seem to delight; Is. 58:2, "Yet they [. . .] delight to know my ways." {They may} delight in hearing the Word; Ezek. 33:31–32, "And they come unto thee as the people cometh, and they sit before thee as my people, and they hear thy words, but they will not do them: for with their mouth they show much love, but their heart goeth after their covetousness. And, lo, thou art unto them as a very lovely song of one that hath a pleasant voice, and can play well on an instrument: for they hear they words, but them do them not." [As] Herod—Mark. 6:20, "For Herod feared John, knowing he was a just man and an holy, and observed him; and when he heard him, he did many things, and heard him gladly." [Many] rejoiced in his light; John 5:35, "He was a burning and shining light: and ye were willing for a season to rejoice in his light."

Many that are not really converted, may make an appearance of conversion by expressly professing to be converted. [The] Pharisees of old professed themselves to be saints, [as did] Simon Magus, [and] many others.

[They] may profess all those things that belong to conversion. [There] may be outward appearances of great affection in their profession, and in their performances of religious duties. [They may be] very affectionate in prayer. Is. 58:4, cause "your voice to be heard on high."

[They] may with appearances of great affection bless and praise God. Mark 2:12, "And immediately he arose, took up the bed, and went forth before them all: insomuch that they were all amazed, and glorified God, saying, We never saw it on this fashion." Matt. 15:31, "Insomuch that the multitude wondered, when they saw the dumb to speak, the maimed to be whole, the lame to walk, and the blind to see: and they glorified the God of Israel." Luke 7:16, "And there came a fear on all: and they glorified God, saying, That a great prophet is risen up among us; and, That God hath visited his people." Luke 4:15, "And he taught in their synagogues, being glorified of all." [Matt. 21:9, "And the multitudes that went before, and that followed, cried, saying,] Hosanna to the Son of David: Blessed is he that cometh in the name of the Lord: Hosanna in the highest." Acts 13:48, "And when the gentiles heard this, they were glad, and glorified the word of the Lord: and as many as were ordained to eternal life believed."

[They] may with great seeming affection call upon others to glorify God. {They may call} upon all the world. Dan. 3:28–30,

> Then Nebuchadnezzar spake, and said, Blessed be the God of Shadrach, Meshach, and Abednego, who hath sent his angel, and delivered his servants that trusted in him, and have changed the king's word, and yielded their bodies, that they might not serve nor worship any god, except their own God. Therefore I make a decree, That every people, nation, and language, which speak anything amiss against the God of Shadrach, Meshach, and Abednego, shall be cut in pieces, and their houses shall be made a dunghill: because there is no other God that can deliver after this sort. Then the king promoted Shadrach, Meshach, and Abednego, in the province of Babylon.

And 4:1–3, "Nebuchadnezzar the king, unto all the people, nations, and languages, that dwell in all the earth; Peace be multiplied unto you. I thought it good to show the signs and wonders that the high God hath wrought toward me. How great are his signs! and how mighty are his wonders! his kingdom is an everlasting kingdom, and his dominion is from generation to generation." [Vv.] 34–35, "And at the end of the days I Nebuchadnezzar lifted up mine eyes unto heaven, and mine understanding returned unto me, and I blessed the most High, and I praised and honored him that liveth forever, whose dominion is an everlasting dominion, and his kingdom is from generation to generation: and all the inhabitants of the earth are reputed as nothing: and he doeth according to his will in the army of heaven, and among the inhabitants of the earth: and none can stay his hand, or say unto him, What doest thou?" [V.] 37, "Now I Nebuchadnezzar praise and extol and honor the King of heaven, all whose works are truth, and his ways judgment: and those that walk in pride he is able to abase." And 6:25–27, "Then king Darius wrote unto all people, nations, and languages, that dwell in all the earth; Peace be multiplied unto you. I make a decree, That in every dominion of my kingdom men tremble and fear before the God of Daniel: for he is the living God, and steadfast forever, and his kingdom that which shall not be destroyed, and his dominion shall be even unto the end. He delivereth and rescueth, and he worketh signs and wonders in heaven and in earth, who hath delivered Daniel from the power of the lions. So this Daniel prospered in the reign of Darius, and in the reign of Cyrus the Persian."

[Many that are not really converted are] forward to talk {of religion and to} tell their experience. {They are} fluent, fervent and abundant in religious talk. In this respect [they] draw near to God with their lips, {and} with [their] mouth show much love.[11] A barren tree may have many leaves. A cloud may look black {and threatening, and} may come with a strong wind, and yet there be no rain. Prov. 25:14, "Whoso boasteth [himself of a false gift is like clouds and wind without rain]." II Pet 2:17, "These are wells without water, clouds that are carried with a tempest; to whom the mist of darkness is reserved forever."[12] Jude, v. 4, "For there are certain men crept in unawares, who were before of old ordained to the condemnation, ungodly men, turning the grace of our God into lasciviousness, and denying the only Lord God, and our Lord Jesus Christ." And [v.] 12, "These are spots in your feasts of charity, when they feast with you, feeding themselves without fear: clouds they are without water, carried about of winds; trees whose fruit withereth, without fruit, twice dead, plucked up by the roots."

All external appearances may be such, that the most discerning eye may not be able [to discern]. The Law of Moses supposes there to be some cases wherein the priest, by all that appeared at present, could not possibly discern whether a man was leprous or clean, Lev. 13. All judging of others' state is uncertain, as is implied by I Sam. 16:7, "The Lord seeth not as man seeth: for man looketh on the outward appearance, but the Lord looketh on the heart." Is. 11:3, "he shall not judge after the sight of his eyes."

If Christ himself were to judge only by outward [appearances, then many that are really unconverted would have to be accepted as true].

'Tis said of that which of old was called tares, {do not gather them in while they grow, "lest while ye gather up the tares, ye root up also the

11. A paraphrase of Is. 29:13.

12. JE writes: "Those are clouds without w. driven," which more closely parallels the words of Jude 12, quoted at the end of this paragraph. Therefore, the phrasing of II Pet. 2:17 is provided here.

wheat with them. Let both grow together until the harvest: and in the time of harvest . . . say to the reapers, Gather ye together first the tares, and bind them in bundles to burn them: but gather the wheat into my barn}" [Matt. 13:29–30].

Especially are there many in a time of great outpouring of the Spirit, when so many things concur {between those that are truly converted and those who are not}, that have great appearances {of true conversion}. A time of great outpouring {of the Spirit} is like the springtime, when the flowers appear, and the trees are in the blossom. But among those blossoms, it is impossible for the most discerning person certainly to distinguish [which will bear fruit, and which not]. The greatest appearances of grace have failed, and the best judges have been deceived. We have an instance of both in David, with respect to Ahithophel, Ps. 55:12–13. "For it was not an enemy that reproached me; then I could have borne it: neither was it he that hated me that did magnify himself against me; then I would have hid myself from him: but it was thou, a man mine equal, my guide, and mine acquaintance." Thus there are many that are not really converted, that yet seem to be converted, by the external appearances there are of conversion.

*Second.* Many that are not truly {converted}, seem {to be truly converted} by internal resemblances {they have to true saints}.

It is certain that there is a vast difference between all that hypocrites experience, and those things that are experienced by true saints. The Scripture represents {this abundantly}. It is also certain that there may be in many things a very great resemblance.

I would therefore endeavor to state this matter, as justly as the so narrow a compass of the present discourse will allow, first, by showing wherein there may be a very great similitude and resemblance between those internal exercises and experiences of hypocrites and true converts; and second, wherein there is no resemblance, but an exceeding great difference.

1. {Show wherein there may be a very great similitude and resemblance between those internal exercises and experiences of hypocrites and true converts}.

(1) There may be a similitude as to the number and variety of sorts of graces and experiences.

[They] may have awakenings and convictions.

[They may have] experiences [that are] preparatory.

[They may have] counterfeits of spiritual knowledge.

(2) Those experiences and seeming graces {that hypocrites experience} may, in their general nature, be exactly like [the experiences of true converts].

'Tis not everything that belongs to true grace or saving experience, that is peculiar. Those things that belong to the general nature [of true converts, belong to the experiences of hypocrites]. It may be illustrated by this: There is a vast difference between the human nature, and the nature of beasts. But yet {their general nature has much in common}.

Thus there is a great deal belonging to saving graces and experiences. [They have their] seat in the same faculties. [They] have the same general names. [They are] truly called by the name of "gratitude." And as they are properly called by the same general names, so there are many things belonging to their nature and operations, common affections and gracious affections, that are the very same. Thus, for instance, a natural man's love to a near relation in many respects has the same operation [in a regenerate man]. [Their] general nature is the same.

(3) The means and manner and circumstances of the production of the experiences and counterfeit graces {in hypocrites}, may be in many respects the same [as in those who are truly converted]. {So the} means of grace, [the] providences of God.

[They are] not produced by themselves. [They are] without any design or contrivance of theirs. Yea, both may be by the Spirit of God. [They may come] by texts of Scripture coming suddenly to mind.

(4) There may be an exact resemblance as to method and order. There is nothing spiritual or divine in the order of time.

(5) There may be great resemblances in the degree. Gal. 4:15, "Where is then the blessedness ye spake of? for I bear you record, that, if it had been possible, ye would have plucked out your own eyes, and have given them to me." V. 11, Paul was afraid of 'em, [lest he had bestowed upon them labor in vain]. [So the Israelites] at the Red Sea. {So those who cried,} "Hosanna!"

(6) [There may be great resemblances in] many of the effects. [In the] opinions they have of themselves. [They have] great consideration [of themselves]. "Are we blind also?" (John 9:40). "God, I thank thee, [that I am not as other men are, extortioners, unjust, adulterers, or even as this publican," Luke 18:11].

2. Wherein there is no resemblance. Three things:

(1) The nature of the operation and influence of the Spirit of God that produces them.

[The nature is] spiritual, supernatural and divine. [It is a] creating something anew.

Infusing new principles. [Whereas] in natural men, {it is} only as cooperating with natural principles.

[The Spirit of God is] as [an] indwelling, vital principle, united, communicating himself. [Whereas] in natural men, not so.

(2) [They are] totally different [one] from another, as to the particular nature and essence of 'em.

It was observed before, that {there are resemblances between the true convert and the hypocrite}, as to their general nature. But in the saving graces of the true saint, there is besides the general nature {a special principle}.

As in the nature of men [there are resemblances, yet in true converts there is] besides {something different}.

There may be such a general agreement between the affections that are in hypocrites and those that are the true saints, that they may have the same general denomination, {and} the same general operations, and yet the particular nature {of their experience is} entirely diverse, [having] nothing common in it.

Some things are common to gracious affections with other affections.

Thus a saint's love to God, may have many things appertaining to it, which are common to a natural man's love to a near relation. But yet the particular and essential nature of a saint's love to God, [is] totally diverse. That idea he has of God's loveliness, that sensation, [is totally diverse].

Both cause desires {in hypocrites and true converts}, but they are not the same sort of desires.

Both {cause} delight, {but they are not the same sort}.

It may be clearly illustrated by this: We will suppose two men; the one is born without the sense of tasting, {the other has it. They may both love the} same delicious sorts of fruit, that is both beautiful to the eye and of a peculiar, exquisitely sweet taste, [but the one loves it for its color, the other for its taste]. In these respects there is no resemblance, [but] a great contrariety.[13]

13. This illustration is taken from *Religious Affections* (WJE 2:209); the insertions

(3) {There is no resemblance} in their most essential effects:

[They] bring the soul to a devotedness to God.

[They] make God their highest end.

[They] forsake all for him.

[They] sincerely comply to an universal obedience.

[They comply to] the fixing of the soul in a way of obedience.

['Tis a] causing the soul to take its rest and contentment in God.

[They] engage it in seeking God above all things.

Thus true saints are distinguished from them that are only wolves in sheep's clothing, by their fruits: for men do not gather grapes of thorns, nor figs of thistles [Matt. 7:16].

## APPLICATION.

Since it is so, {that there are many persons that seem to be converted, that are not so really}, let all be exhorted to great care, that they ben't deceived about themselves as to this matter.

That there are so many {resemblances between hypocrites and true converts}, thence the great danger there is of men's being deceived. And what has been observed of the great and manifold resemblances {between them}, shows the straitness of the gate; and does yet more fully show how liable men are to be deceived, and what great need there is of care, and the utmost strictness and diligence, of watchfulness and inquiry, lest we be deceived.

Consider further,

*First*. How many things there are that do concur to increase men's liableness to be deceived, besides the manifold and great false appearances there are of conversion.

The great prejudices there are in our hearts to blind us.

A fondness from self-love of such a persuasion.

How evident is this in mankind.

And how apt are men to be deceived concerning their own practices and dispositions, through the pride of the heart. How very manifest is this. [They] diminish what is against 'em, magnify what seems to look well on them. You have the same heart in these respects that others have.

And besides all this, there is the management of a most subtil and crafty adversary, the grand deceiver of mankind. How much superior is

---

are based on JE's wording there.

his subtilty to our wisdom. What advantages he has. How he transforms himself [into an angel of light]. How much he carries on his designs against miserable mankind, by mimicking the works of God. How much experience he has had. How indefatigable he is. How successful a deceiver of mankind he has been in many respects.

*Second*. How hard it is for those that have once established an opinion of themselves as true converts, on false grounds, to be brought off from their delusion.

Prejudices from self-love have here a more powerful influence than in inducing men first to take up a false hope. Men's self-love may so dispose 'em to lay hold on that which they are fond of, that don't belong to 'em, that it may be hard to keep 'em from it. But it makes it much harder to bring men to part with that that they are very fond of, and have long been in possession of, and thought was their own. 'Tis hard to bring men off from a false hope, after they continued in it sometime: for by this means, everything that appertains to their false hope becomes habitual to 'em, such as their security, their comfort, that quietness and false peace of mind that they have.

These things, by being remaining, are more and more rooted; as an ill plant that is long let alone, it grows greater and stronger, and is more and more deeply rooted in the ground. [It is] hardly[14] rooted out.

A false hope is like many chronical distempers, {that make persons abundantly more susceptive}.[15]

A false hope, by men's continuing long in it, does very much put men beyond the means of conviction of their miserable state. Conviction {of our miserable state} is by the enlightening and awakening the conscience. But stupefying nature exceedingly so [prevents conviction].

And then, many of those that are deceived {about their conversion}, have the charitable opinion of others to strengthen them {in their opinion}. It may be the duty of others to receive many of those that are not really true converts into their charity, from the profession {they make} and appearances {they give}. And there is multitudes [who], on undue forwardness, {are received into charity, and} from slight appearances. But few make proper distinction. But few are aware. Hence many that are deceived are under great disadvantages.

14. I.e., with difficulty.

15. The insertion is taken from *Religious Affections* (WJE 2:213), where JE used the same simile in explaining "imaginary ideas."

*Third*. Consider how dreadful a thing a false hope is to live and die by. It may serve persons while [they] live to some purposes, or maintain a false peace. [It may] cause such a show as may gain them credit and honor in the world. But it will not stand by 'em long. Their building will fall. [They may] lean upon their house, but great will be the fall.

It does 'em no real good while they live. [It] makes 'em truly much more miserable; exceedingly gives the devil advantage against every man, to exercise his tyranny over 'em without control. It keeps an open door for him. It is a strong fort for Satan in the soul. It hardens the heart; emboldens in sin; feeds pride; treasures up wrath, and causes that, at last, destruction comes with more terrible surprise.

[As the] rich man in hell. [He was] a child of Abraham [Luke 16:19–31].

We read of fearfulness that shall surprise the hypocrite [Is. 33:14]. A more dreadful wrath comes on them than others. Is. 10:6, "people of my wrath."

So that the consequences of a false hope are every way fatal and dreadful. Those that are settled in a false hope, are in an inexpressibly doleful condition. [They are] much more unlikely to [be] converted, than those that have been bred up in the grossest heathenism. The ignorant, barbarous Indians are more likely {to be converted than they}.

Those that have long been established through false experiences, high imaginations [and] common affections, are perhaps next to those that have committed the unpardonable sin.

Let the consideration of these things, together [with] what was mentioned before, excite all, as they would have any regard to their own eternal welfare, to the utmost care {that they are not settled in a false hope}.

I will conclude my discourse on this Doctrine, with some advice with respect to the method that you should take, as you would not be deceived in a matter of such infinite concern.

1. Don't rest in any of those appearances of grace, either outward or inward, that you have heard may be found in them that are not converted.

2. Don't depend on the judgment of men.

Many depend on the doctrines they teach and make manifest from the Word of God.

Praise [is] not of men, [but of God, Rom. 2:29].

['Tis a] light thing to be judged. I Cor. 4:5, "[Therefore judge nothing before the time, until the Lord come, who both will bring to light the hidden things of darkness, and will make manifest the counsels of the hearts: and then shall every man have praise of God]."

3. Rest in nothing as a certain evidence of grace but what is beyond all that ever was, as well as can be, experienced by natural men, either in this world or that which is to come.

True saints have those experiences that [are beyond those of natural men].

We read in the Scriptures many things that had a great show of virtue in natural men. [As] Saul; I Sam. 24:16, etc.,

> [And it came to pass, when David had made an end of speaking these words unto Saul, that Saul said, Is this thy voice, my son David? And Saul lifted up his voice, and wept. And he said to David, Thou art more righteous than I: for thou hast rewarded me good, whereas I have rewarded thee evil. And thou hast showed this day how that thou hast dealt well with me: forasmuch as when the Lord had delivered me into thine hand, thou killedst me not. For if a man find his enemy, will he let him go well away? wherefore the Lord reward thee good for that thou hast done unto me this day. And now, behold, I know well that thou shalt surely be king, and that the kingdom of Israel shall be established in thine hand.]

Ch. 26:21, "Then said Saul, I have sinned: return, my son David: for I will no more do thee harm, because my soul was precious in thine eyes this day: behold, I have played the fool, and have erred exceedingly."

Therefore, don't rest in what is no more than {the experience of natural men}. [So] Nebuchadnezzar; Dan. 2:47, "The king answered unto Daniel, and said, Of a truth it is, that your God is a God of gods, and a Lord of kings, and a revealer of secrets, seeing thou couldest reveal this secret." Ch. 4, at the beginning,[16] "Nebuchadnezzar the king, unto all people, nations, and languages, that well in all the earth; Peace be multiplied unto you. I thought it good to show the signs and wonders that the high God hath wrought toward me. How great are his signs! and how mighty are his wonders! his kingdom is an everlasting kingdom, and his dominion is from generation to generation." Vv. 34, etc., "And at the end of the days I Nebuchadnezzar lifted up mine eyes unto heaven, and

---

16. MS: "3. 4. <at the beginning>."

mine understanding returned unto me, and I blessed the most High, and I praised and honored him that liveth forever, whose dominion is an everlasting dominion, and his kingdom is from generation to generation: and all the inhabitants of the earth are reputed as nothing: and he doeth according to his will in the army of heaven, and among the inhabitants of the earth: and none can stay his hand, or say unto him, What doest thou?" Dan. 6:25, etc., "Then king Darius wrote unto all people, nations, and languages, that dwell in all the earth; Peace be multiplied unto you. I make a decree, That in every dominion of my kingdom men tremble and fear before the God of Daniel: for he is the living God, and steadfast forever, and his kingdom that which shall not be destroyed, and his dominion shall be even unto the end. He delivereth and rescueth, and he worketh signs and wonders in heaven and in earth, who hath delivered Daniel from the power of the lions." [So] the children of Israel at the Red Sea [Ex. 15:1–19]; Judas [Luke 22:47–48]; the multitude that saw Christ's miracles;[17] [and] those that cried, Hosanna [Matt. 21:9].

Such as are spoken of, Heb. 6[:1–8]. Such [judgment] natural men will experience in another world, at the day of judgment.

4. Don't all your days rest chiefly in your first work. This is unscriptural. Signs are given.

This [is] not chiefly insisted on in Scripture. Other things that are experienced in a course are much more insisted on.

[It is] contrary to the method we are instructed in in Scripture: run as not uncertainly, press forward, give diligence. If there be any good reason for your so doing, it must be one of these two: either that the order of things in the first work, is a thing that may safely and surely be depended on; or that the nature of things is better seen in the experience of a few minutes, than in a repetition and series of experiences through a course. As to the former, ['tis imprudent to trust in it]. As to the latter, [the expense may be transient].

By conversing with Christ forty days.

Many infallible proofs.

'Tis very unsafe for persons to trust mainly {in their first work}, on this account: grace is much more likely to be counterfeited with great resemblance by the new affections that arise on some sudden change, and new apprehension and impression that a person passes under, than in the views and affections that [are] often repeated. A sudden change

17. John 6:2 and elsewhere.

by common illumination or delusion of Satan, after great exercise and fears of hell, that gives hope {of conversion}, naturally excites exceeding high affections.

[They are owing to] the novelty of things.

And when counterfeit religious affections are very high, there is in many respects a much greater resemblance of grace. More things are sensible and experienced together, in such a case, that are like grace. There is such a concatenation of affections, that one affection, when it is raised very high, sets all the rest in motion. So that there may be an appearance of many graces together.

When persons are highly affected by a new hope {of conversion}, they may easily be deceived about their hearts. Saul, when highly affected, thought he was become David's friend. [He was] disposed to treat him as such. [The] children of Israel, when highly affected at Mount Sinai, thought they found a heart to cleave to God. The Galatians {were highly affected by Paul's preaching, but then followed other teachers}.

So persons, when, after great fears {of hell}, they are highly affected by some sudden change, easily are deceived about the disposition of their hearts towards God. [They] think they love God above all; see him to be better than all; [are] willing to do and suffer all things for his sake. 'Tis apparent in such, that it is so.

Hence {they think they are} willing to be damned.

[The] reason [is] easily to be seen: that affection swallows up [everything else] at that time. They don't then feel their contrary affections. Hence [they] think sometimes that they shall never sin anymore; [they would] rather die, [or] burn at the stake.

Therefore, it will be very imprudent in you to trust mainly to your first work.

5. Rest in nothing but that which you find to be habitual, neither [a] first work nor any other transient, high affections or impressions.

This is evidently the scriptural way. 'Tis not this nor that transient thing, but a new creature. 'Tis not so much he that thinks he has loved, {but} he that loves. He that is pure in heart. He that loves the brethren.

6. Let it be what you earnestly seek, that there may always be maintained in you an enlightened and awakened sense.

The means that God makes use of to undeceive hypocrites is by [conviction].

This is the way that hypocrites will be undeceived at the day of judgment. The main reason why those that are deceived are so remediless, as they are {by nature, is that they} stupefy their consciences.

Therefore [seek an enlightened and awakened sense].

7. Rest in no experiences but those that you find have this nature and tendency, to increase awakenings and convictions of conscience.

I don't mean to increase terror. There is a great difference.

Awakenings and convictions of conscience consist in [conviction of sinfulness of heart and practice, and of the dreadfulness of sin, as committed against a God of terrible majesty, infinite holiness and hatred of sin, and strict justice in punishing of it.][18]

And it is the tendency [of awakenings and convictions to convince of sin].

There are many sorts of experiences that have a directly contrary tendency.

All false comforts have a contrary tendency.

Rest in no experiences but those that convince you more of your sinfulness.

Spiritual light has a vastly greater tendency to this, than anything that natural men [can have].

8. Rest in no experiences but those that you find increase a sense of your needs:

[Those that make you] more poor in spirit, more of a beggar.

[Those that] show you more your distance from what you ought to be, and need to be.

9. Rest in no experiences but those that you find increase appetite and a spirit of engagedness in seeking God.

Herein chiefly consists Christian zeal, which is the very thing that distinguishes true Christians from lukewarm professors, viz., in this fervent and engaged spirit in[19] the work of a Christian. Tit. 2:14, "zealous of good works." This zeal is here spoken of as the very end of the great work of redemption; and therefore undoubtedly all that is done in that work, and all that is purchased in it, and all that grace that is bestowed in the application of redemption, has a tendency hereto.[20]

18. The insert is taken from *Religious Affections*, pt. II, no. 8 (WJE 2:156).

19. MS: "sp. of in."

20. The third preaching unit ends here.

## [DOCTRINE RESUMED.]
### OBSERVATION IV.

*Wicked men cannot always enjoy their element but must, first and last,*
*be forever separated from it.*

Indeed, the text speaks only of those wicked men that are in some sort enclosed in Christ's net, i.e., within the limits of his visible kingdom. But this parable has a direct regard only to them, when it speaks of the bad fish being drawn to shore out of the water, and being cast away; and so in the explanation of the parable, of the wicked's being cast into a furnace of fire. Yet we are not to understand the parable exclusive of others, as though those wicked men only who are {drawn to shore and cast away}, should be cast into a furnace of fire. And if we take the parable as having a regard only to those that are in the visible kingdom of Christ, and under means, it equally and indeed more especially concerns us, as it shows the misery of all wicked men amongst us: for we all are some of those that are enclosed in Christ's net, in that respect, that we are within the limits of Christendom, and under the appointed means of grace and salvation.

I have already observed under a former observation, that the enjoyments of this world, and the objects of their lusts, are natural men's element. I now proceed to show,

[*First.*] Natural men can't always enjoy this their element, but must leave it.

*Second.* That they must be so separated from it, as never to return to it anymore.

*First.* Natural men cannot always enjoy the things of this world as their element, but the time will come when they leave it. And that either, first, they must forsake and renounce it in conversion; or second, they must be forced from it by being taken out of the world.

1. Some that are now in a natural state, and whose element is the world, will be as it were brought out of it by conversion.

When a sinner is converted, he changes his element. A sinner, when he is converted, changes his element, as being taken out of it. He never would forsake it of his own accord, if left to himself. 'Tis a great change that is wrought by the mighty power, and according to the good pleasure of Jesus Christ. He seizes sinners while swimming in this element and in their career in sin, and stops 'em in their course, and encloses them in his net; and by his power draws them out into another element exceeding diverse from it. This change, in some respect, is sorely against men's wills, and in other respects it is what the wills of those that are the subjects of it do entirely fall in with, and are altogether free and active in. A sinner's conversion is a change altogether against the will of the sinner, but altogether agreeable to the will of the convert.

He that is to [be] converted, so long as he remains a sinner, is opposite to the change; there is nothing can be more contrary to him. He opposes it with all his might. But that moment that he actually becomes the subject of the change, his will therein is altogether free and active.

There are some things that God doth to the sinner in order to his conversion, and that he is the subject of, while he is yet in a state of sin, and so while he is yet in his element. There are divine dispensations and influences of the Spirit that he is the subject of, that have a tendency to his conversion, and are preparatory to it, while the sinner is yet in a natural state. In these, the sinner opposes and resists God, as a fish [resists begin taken from the water]. All the powers of the soul are bent against it—sinners that are awakened, as well as others. There is nothing that a sinner opposes more than conversion, for it is a forsaking his element; [it is to] forsake the world and his own righteousness; 'tis death to him. He opposes it more than hell.

Thus it is, till the moment that these spiritual fish are drawn out of the water. In the moment of a sinner's conversion, his element is changed. His will is changed. In that moment, he is willing. He is a new creature. Conversion itself is never wrought against what is then a man's will. Then, above all things, it becomes agreeable to his will; that which was his death is now his life, and that which was his life and element is now his death. As we see, it is as hard to force land animals under water, as to force fish out of it.

When a sinner is converted, he renounces that which formerly he placed all his happiness in. Those things that he delighted in, and was glued to, become bitter to him. [He] mourns. His nature opposes and strives against it. And now he has a new nature, a new relish. Herein appears the mighty, converting power of God.

2. If natural men don't forsake these worldly things, that are their element, in conversion, the time is coming when they must be forced from them by being taken out of the world.

'Tis evident that one thing intended in the parable we are upon, by the fish being drawn ashore, is that great change in men's state that they pass under when they are removed from the present changeable state, to their fixed and everlasting state. The fish, when drawn ashore, are represented as coming before those that are to judge of 'em, and finally to dispose of 'em, as all men must be removed {at the day of judgment who are found wanting}.

So all those that continue finally in a carnal state, and have the things of this world and the enjoyments of their lusts for their element as long as they live, must then be forcibly separated. When they are come to the appointed limits {of their time}, their separation from {this world} will be unavoidable. Though they have placed all their happiness [here], never relished any other good, saw nothing else in which their souls could be gratified; though they will have no other good to be received to, then their separation {from this world} will be total.

The covetous man shall be rent. The sensualist will in an awful manner be forever rent {from this world}.

Those that shall be alive at Christ's appearance [shall be rent].

*Second.* {That they must be so separated from it, as} never to return to it anymore.

Then they will be their own tormentors. As when a dry tree is cast into the fire, one part kindles another.

## APPLICATION.

[The] *Use* may be of *Warning* to all, to take heed that the misery of the damned ben't their future portion. You have heard something described of the nature of that misery, which, though the description that has been given is very faint and imperfect, yet may serve to convince you that the state of the damned is unspeakably horrible. Therefore, as all have immortal souls, {and} all are naturally exposed {to destruction, so} all are now in a state of probation; and as it is but a little while {before you are separated}, let all now take heed that this dreadful state that you have heard of ben't your eternal portion, {and that} that wailing and gnashing of teeth ben't your eternal employment.

Here, consider further these two things:

*First.* Consider the properties and circumstances of this sorrow and rage.

1. Both their sorrow and rage will[21] be perfect.

[(1)] Sorrow without any mitigation or alleviation, without any comforter, without any pity, no comforting consideration, no relief.

It will be [to] an extreme degree, inconceivably beyond all that men are ever the subjects of in this world.

Sorrow and grief, in many instances, has risen to a great height in this world.

[They have risen to such a height as to] break men's hearts, [to make them] weary of life, [make them] long for death.

[They are] more terrible than extreme bodily torments, so as to destroy the frame of the body.

[They have] quite overwhelmed {the soul}.

But {hereafter, sorrow will be perfect}.

The Psalmist speaks of his sorrow as being like a flood of great waters, waves and billows, water spouts. [He] compares it to the great abyss.

Ps. 42:7,[22] "Deep calleth unto deep at the noise of thy water spouts: all thy waves [and thy billows are gone over me]." But all [this is as] but a drop.

Spiritual sorrows sometimes have been great. Those foretastes that have sometimes been given of the sorrow of the future world [have been great]. But {these are small in comparison to the sorrows of the damned}.

It is a world made for sorrow, the proper, eternal habitation of it, where it may appear in its perfection. Everything is answerably gloomy and horrible. There is "blackness of darkness" [Jude 13]. That is a land of darkness, as darkness itself. There [are] the shadows of death in the highest sense.

The darkness of the grave seems dismal, but {the darkness of hell is perfect}.

Hell is a world appointed as the eternal dwelling place of evil, moral and natural evil, that all may be gathered there, left there forever, [to] reign there.

Things therefore are agreeable to this. That sorrow {in hell that the damned feel} will perfectly sink the soul. There will be no remaining support or courage. Their cup will be mingled by God himself. There

21. MS: "with."
22. MS cites ch. 43.

will be bitter ingredients indeed {in that cup, but} they must drink the very dregs. Ps. 75:8, "in the hand of the Lord is a cup, the wine thereof is red."

[(2)] And as their sorrow will be perfect, so will their rage: for as was observed before, {in hell the damned will have} no restraint. The rage of their lust, their pride, [their] enmity against God, [their] envy and malice, [will have no restraint]. All their power, and the utmost of their capacity, will be exerted.

2. The sorrow and rage {of the damned in hell} will be altogether fruitless. As was observed before, the wicked hereafter will bewail the things that are past. But [it will be] altogether a fruitless sorrow.

So their rage against God and the saints and angels. [They will] gnash their teeth, and melt away [Ps. 112:10].

It being fruitless as to others, they themselves will suffer it; as the flame of their rage reaches not the objects of it, it will only prey on them. The fire, finding no other fuel to kindle on, will consume them. They will gnash with their teeth, but the objects of their malice being out of their reach, they in their gnashing their teeth will bite nothing but their own tongues; which seems to be what is intended, Rev. 16:10, "gnawed their tongues for pain."

And as to their rage against their fellow damned sinners, though it will [only] avail to add to their torment, yet that in the issue will be no benefit to them, but only serve to increase their own misery.

3. The wicked, with all their rage, will not be able to support themselves against the rage that will be against them. As their corruption, so their pride and envy and malice will rage against God.

So there are other things that will rage against them. Hell [. . .][23]

## [DOCTRINE RESUMED.]
## OBSERVATION V.

{*The wicked shall*} *not always remain mingled among the righteous.*

[. . .][24]

---

23. MS breaks off. The remainder of the Application for this sermon, and the entirety of the sermon treating Obs. V, are missing. Obs. V, we know from the beginning of the next extant sermon, is, "{The wicked shall} not always remain mingled among the righteous."

24. Lacunae in MS (see previous note).

## OBSERVATION VI.

*This world must come to an end.*[25]

This, He that made the world, has often declared. The extraordinary stability of anything is in Scripture represented by comparing it to the mountain, called [an] "everlasting mountain," Hab. 3:6. But we are told these shall depart, Is. 54:10. [We] are told the heavens shall wax old. Ps. 102:25–26, "Of old hast thou laid the foundation of the earth: and the heavens are the work of thy hands. They shall perish, but thou shalt endure: yea, all of them shall wax old like a garment; as a vesture shalt thou change them, and they shall be changed." {We are told that the} stars shall fall from heaven. Rev. 6:13–14, "And the stars of heaven fell unto the earth, even as a fig tree casteth her untimely figs, when she is shaken of a mighty wind. And the heaven departed as a scroll when it is rolled together; and every mountain and island were moved out of their places." All these things [shall] be dissolved. II Pet. 3:10–11, "But the day of the Lord will come as a thief in the night; in the which the heavens shall pass away with a great noise, and the elements shall melt with fervent heat, the earth also and the works that are therein shall be burned up. Seeing then that all these things shall be dissolved, what manner of persons ought ye to be in all holy conversation and godliness." And indeed, that this world will come to an end, may be argued from its nature.

The changes that are in the world, especially some of them, are forerunners of its destruction. [There are] changes on earth, changes in the heavens. And not only those extraordinary changes, but its continual changes [and] revolutions. They are as it were so many steps of its progress towards its end.

God's chariot, Ezek. 1, sits in the firmament, v. 26; rides in the heavens. Deut. 33:26, "There is none like unto the God of Jeshurun, who rideth upon the heaven in thy help, and in his excellency on the sky." Revolutions are the motions of the wheels towards the journey's end.

---

25. JE outlined and then deleted the following:

OBS. VI. *When the full number of the elect shall be gathered in, the world will soon come to an end.*
1. This world must come to an end.
2. The full number of the elect must be gathered in.
3. When this is done, the world will soon come to an end.
I. *Prop.* This world must come to an end.
By "the world," I mean not only this earth.

'Tis very manifest that the world is made but for a temporary use, made for the inhabitants,[26] Is. 45:18, created to be inhabited: "For thus saith the Lord that created the heavens; God himself that formed the earth and made it; he hath established it, he created it not in vain, he formed it to be inhabited." [It is made] chiefly for men. 'Tis manifest that this is no settled abode of mankind.

So that the evidence that this world will come to an end, is very abundant.

But then, for the rightly understanding of this, I would briefly observe a few things:

[*First.*] *Negatively.*

1. 'Tis not intended that the world will be annihilated, or return to its first nothing. Expressions used import the contrary. [The heavens shall] wax old {as a garment} [Ps. 102:26].

2. The inhabitants of the world shall not all cease to be.

[*Second.*] But *Affirmatively,*

1. That the frame of the world shall utterly be destroyed. God made the matter of the world before he constituted its frame. This shall be wholly destroyed, dissolved, as it were dashed in pieces; destroyed, as that which is old and useless. "The furnace of the earth, [purified seven times," Ps. 12:6]. "[The] mountains [shall be molten under him, and the] valleys [shall be cleft," Mic. 1:4]. Rivers [shall] cease to flow. [The] sea [shall be turned into] dry land.

[There will] no longer be such an expanse of air, [with] clouds and vapors suspended in it, [and] such a variety of seasons. [There will be] an end to the produce of the earth, [an] end of all living things in it; but only mankind [will survive].

Not only the frame of the earth, but the visible heavens, shall be a total and perfect destruction. There is no way by which the frame and contexture of things can be more perfectly destroyed, than by their being thrown into the fire and burnt up. But {this is what shall happen to the earth and heaven}.

2. Then will be a total and eternal end to the state of mankind in the world. [There will be an] end to the present habitations of men, all their buildings, palaces, cities, towns.

All the works of mankind [shall end]. Here [consider], II Pet. 3:10, "The earth, with all the works that are therein, shall be burnt up." And

26. MS: "Inhabited."

[then shall come an] end to all things appertaining to the civil state of mankind: all civil societies, kingdoms, empires, commonwealths, provinces, corporations; all civil offices and honors and distinctions, all civil relations.

[Then will come an] end to all human laws, all civil rights and privileges, all civil conventions, parliament, courts of judicature; all negotiation, administrations; all affairs of the world relating to peace and war.

[Then will come the] destruction of all weapons of war, fortresses.

[Then will come] an end to the present ecclesiastical state of the professing world, all ecclesiastical societies, officers, church processes.

[Then will come an end] to the present state of mankind as to their family state and relations.

[Then will come to] an end to all worldly business, husbandry, commerce, merchandize.

[Then will come to an end] navigation, ships of the sea.

[Then will come to an end] all mechanical, or trades, or handicraft employment.

[Then will come] an end of the present state of the persons of men, [the] state of their bodies. [Their bodies will] no more subsist by meat, drink and clothing; [they] will pass under an exceeding great change, whereby they will become immortal.

The bodies of the righteous will {be raised incorruptible [I Cor. 15:52]}. The bodies of the wicked {will be cast into the lake of fire}. And the circumstances of their souls will be very different: no longer in a state of probation, [a] state of imperfection. [They will no longer be in an] intermediate state, a state of mixture of good and evil.

3. There will be an end to all that is good and desirable in this world.

As to the persons that are good, they will cease to be any longer in the world. With them, all spiritual good will be removed. [There will remain] no such thing as any piety or virtue, [or] influences of the Spirit of God: [no] conversion, sanctification, [or] divine comforts. [There will be] no more times of outpouring [of the Spirit, or] anything tending to spiritual good: convictions, {or the} means of grace.

[There will be] an end to all temporal good, all worldly profit and wealth, honor, ease and pleasure.

No more of the goodness of God in the world, every stream dried up.

And [an] end to all those things that [had] the shadow and appearance of good, the [things which were] falsely supposed to be good.

[An end to] the carnal ease, all self-righteousness, false comforts, false hopes.

## APPLICATION.

[The Use is of] *Exhortation* to all, to improve this time while they are in the world, to make sure of being redeemed from the earth.

Woe is denounced [to those who are not redeemed].

The bulk of mankind shall perish.

Some are not of the world. [They are] chosen out of the world, redeemed from the earth.

1. There is provision made.

As there was an ark of old, [so is there one today].

As there was a Zoar, [so there is one today, Gen. 19:22–30].

2. If you have made sure of this, that end of the world, which will be the most terrible to others, will on good grounds be the subject of your most joyful expectation.

*Directions*

1. Seek that you may be taken out of the stock of the first Adam, that is of the earth, and is earthy, and be engrafted [into the stock of the second Adam].

2. See to it that you build your hope of an interest in Christ on a foundation that cannot be moved, on a rock.

[See to it that you have] a faith that is of the operation of God: a thorough conviction, a real change of nature. [A faith] not only [of] heat and profession, but do the things that Christ says, that your religion be of a steadfast nature. There is something given to the elect in this world, that is not of the world, that is of an everlasting nature. [It is a] life that is immortal, [a] spring of living water, [a] comfort and joy which none can take from 'em. [They will] not cease to yield their fruit.

3. Forsake this world in your heart, and let it ascend to another world that shall never come to an end. [You will have an] inheritance incorruptible, [which] cannot be shaken, a kingdom that cannot be moved. Let your treasure, heart and life be hid with Christ in God [Col. 3:3]. Never rest satisfied, till you come to respect heaven as your home.

4. Let all your life here in this [world] be improved as a journey towards that world of everlasting glory.

Let your thoughts be chiefly there. Let all the enjoyments of this world be improved in subordination. Let all the affairs of this world be attended [in subordination].

Be ever found in the way that leads thither.

Travel on in this way, in a laborious and constant manner. Be making progress. Hold out to the end.[27]

[DOCTRINE RESUMED.]
OBSERVATION VII.

*When the full number of the elect shall be gathered in, the end of the world will soon come.*

*First Prop.* There is a certain number that God has from all eternity chosen to be conformed to the image of him.

This is variously and abundantly declared in Scripture. We often read of those that God has chosen to salvation. II Thess. 2:13, "God from the beginning hath chosen you." John 13:18, "I know whom I have chosen." Eph. 1:4, "according as he hath chosen us in him before the foundation [of the world]."

The saints are abundantly spoken of in Scripture under that epithet of "elect." Matt. 24:24, "if it were possible, [they shall deceive the very elect]." Rom. 11:7, "the election hath obtained it." I Pet. 1:2, "Elect according to the foreknowledge of God the Father, through sanctification of the Spirit, unto obedience and the sprinkling of the blood of Jesus Christ."

So Christ often speaks of those that the Father hath given to the Son. John 17:2, "given him power over all flesh, that he should give eternal life to as many as thou hast given him." V. 9, "[I] pray not for [the world, but for] them which thou hast given me." John 6:37, "All that the Father giveth me shall come to me."

And again, we read of those whose names are written in the book of life, Rev. 13:18 and 20:15.

---

27. What was most likely the fifth preaching unit ends here.

As to that which those that are the elect are chosen to, the whole is expressed in that in Rom. 8:29, that they might "be conformed to the image of his Son."

*Second Prop.* The full number of the elect must be gathered in, i.e., they must be {separated from the wicked}.

Though multitudes of mankind will be lost, yet not one [of the redeemed shall be lost]. The election must obtain. Those that are left finally in blindness, are none of them of God's elect. Rom. 11:7, "The election hath obtained it, and the rest were blinded." They that are blinded are only those that are lost. II Cor. 4:3, "if our gospel be hid, [it is hid to them that are lost]."

Christ speaks of such as the Father had given him, as those that should come to him, John 6:37. John 10:16—[Christ will] bring in [the other sheep]. The Apostle declares, Rom 8:29, that whom God did foreknow, "he also did predestinate to be conformed to the image of his Son."

Here is a chain that cannot be broken. The saving mercy of God towards {the elect} reaches from eternity to eternity.

The electing love of God stands as an immoveable foundation of the holiness and salvation of all the elect. II Tim. 2:19, "[the] foundation of God standeth sure."

Therefore, it is a thing most certain. Though there be so great a multitude, though so many of the elect dwell in obscurity, though they are exposed to so many dangers, all will come into being, all will {be gathered in}.

The reason why {the elect} will surely be gathered in, may be seen in the things following:

1. The greatness of God's eternal love to each of the elect secures it.

[(1)] The greatness of the love of the Father. This appears by {his giving his Son for the elect}.

[(2)] The greatness of the love of Christ. This appears {by his giving himself for the elect}. This love of Christ is to each individual. Gal. 2:20, "I am crucified with Christ: nevertheless I live; yet not I, but Christ liveth in me: and the life which I now live in the flesh I live by the faith of the Son of God, who loved me, and gave himself for me."

2. God's eternal gift and promise to his Son secures it.

[This was] actually promised before the world began, Tit. 1:2. [It was] as it were already actually given them, II Tim. 1:9. [It was] given us in Christ Jesus before the world began.

3. The immutability of God makes it secure.

4. The great prize that has been paid for their redemption makes it sure.

Otherwise, the blood of Christ would be lost, [his] labors and sufferings frustrated.

5. Christ's concern for his own honor in his office and undertaking.

6. Christ mystical is not complete without [the church], Eph. 1:23.[28]

7. There is no want of sufficiency in God and Christ in order to it.

[In God is] sufficiency of knowledge. [He] knows who are his. [There is] no danger of [their] being overlooked.

[In God is] sufficiency of power. All things are in his hands, all means, all enemies.

8. Christ's exaltation on their account, on their behalf, put him in a proper capacity to gather 'em in.

9. Christ's intercession secures it.

"I pray not for these alone" [John 17:20].

10. The cares Christ took to bring in each elect person when on earth, is an end of it.

[Such as] the woman {who anointed Christ with ointment from an alabaster box}, Luke 7:36–50; [the] woman of Canaan [Matt. 15:22–28]; Zacchaeus [Luke 19:2–10]; the Gadarene [Mark 5:1–20]; [and the] thief on the cross [Luke 23:39–43].

*Third Prop.* When this is done, the end of the world will soon come.

God will send forth his angels. Then shall the end come.

This truth may be illustrated by the following considerations:

1. That woe is denounced to this world. [It is] devoted to destruction.

2. The wrath of God is continually provoked by the immense wickedness that the world is full of.

3. 'Tis abundantly manifest from the Scriptures, that impending judgments and destruction is withheld from the wicked, very much from regard to the elect.

[As was the case with] Sodom. If ten righteous [were found, God would not destroy the city], when it don't appear there were more than one. [Yet God's threatening] counted nothing till he was secure [Gen. 18:16—19:23].

---

28. MS cites Eph. 2:23.

God did not destroy the old [world till] Noah's family was provided for. 'Tis probably not so much as one [was lost]. [They are] spoken of as those that "stand in the gap," and "make up the hedge," Ezek. 22:30.

For Moses' sake, God often turned away his wrath. Ps. 106:23, "Therefore he said that he would destroy them, had not Moses his chosen stood before him in the breach, to turn away his wrath, lest he should destroy them."

[The elect are] spoken of as the defense of a people. "The chariots of Israel, and the horsemen thereof," II Kgs. 2:12; and 13:14, "Now Elisha was fallen sick of his sickness whereof he died. And Joash the king of Israel came down unto him, and wept over his face, and said, O my father, my father, the chariot of Israel, and the horsemen thereof."

It was from regard to the presence of Jehoshaphat [that Elisha listened to the king of Israel], II Kgs. 3:14.

When God was angry with Jerusalem, and was about to destroy it, he says, as in Jer. 5:1, "Run ye to and fro [through the streets of Jerusalem, and see now, and know, and seek in the broad places thereof, if ye can find a man, if there by any that executeth judgment, that seeketh the truth; and I will pardon it]." Ezek. 22:30–31, "And I sought for a man among them, that should make up the hedge, and stand in the gap before me for the land, that I should not destroy it: but I found none. Therefore have I poured out mine indignation upon them; I have consumed them with the fire of my wrath: their own way have I recompensed upon their heads, saith the Lord God."

It was for the elect's sake that a full end was not made. It was for their sakes, from time to time, that that nation was not utterly destroyed. Is. 65:8, "Destroy it not; for a blessing is in it." So God says concerning this wicked world. In this sense, the saints are the salt of the earth.

4. The good things of this world are chiefly for the sake of the elect. "All things are for your sakes" [II Cor. 4:15]. [The] meek [shall] inherit the earth [Matt. 5:5].

5. Were it not for the church of God in the world, the world would soon be in such a state, as not to be fit to stand any longer.

6. This lower world is continued in being, chiefly that it may be the stage on which the work of redemption should be carried on. "Then cometh the end, [when he shall have delivered up the kingdom to God, even the Father; when he shall have put down all rule and all authority and power,]" I Cor. 15:24.

## APPLICATION.

[*Use*] I [of] *Information.*

*First.* Hence the high value that God sets on the elect.

[The elect are] blessings wherever they are.

How great the wickedness of the world is. How God has borne [that wickedness]. How great [has been] his goodness bestowed. How great deliverances has he[29] wrought.

*Second.* Hence learn the unreasonableness of the opposition and enmity of the world against the saints.

*Use* II of *Exhortation.*

*First.* Give all diligence to make your election sure. [This] shows the unspeakable privilege.

The *Direction* that I would give in order it, is this: Make sure of it, that there be in your [heart] a true election or choice of divine things.

Make sure of it, that you do indeed make choice of God as your portion.

[Make sure that you make choice] of Christ as your Savior. Choose [him] in all his offices, in a manner agreeable to his election of his saints: [choose him] above others; with a great love; for special nearness; to be conformed to them; [and] to dwell with them.

Make sure of it, that heaven be your chosen abode, your elect home.

Make sure of it, [that] the way to heaven be your elect path.

Make sure of it, that the people of God be yours.

*Second.* Let those that have evidences of being some of the elect of God, behave themselves as becomes those that stand in the gap.

Become more holy. Eminent saints especially are a defense.

Be much in prayer for the world. Be much in prayer for that glorious increase of the number of the saints.

Endeavor to refrain [from] the wickedness of the world: [heed] instruction, testimony, [and] reproof.

[Endeavor] to promote holiness by your utmost endeavors and influence, by your example.

Herein you will be a sharer in Abraham's high honor and privilege, to whom God promised that he should be blessed, and should be a blessing [Gen. 24:1].[30]

---

29. MS: "has."

30. What was most likely the sixth preaching unit ends here.

## [DOCTRINE RESUMED.]

[The text is] Matt. 13:47–50, [but especially that part of v. 48,] ". . . and gathered the good into vessels . . ."[31]

## OBSERVATION VIII.

*God will hereafter deal with the righteous, as men are wont to treat that*
*which they prize as the portion they live upon.*

In this parable, Christ alludes to what appertained to the occupation of his disciples. They depended on the fish they caught for a subsistence.

*First Prop.* The righteous are God's precious portion.

1. The righteous are precious in God's eyes. This God declares, Is. 43:4, "Since thou wast precious in my sight, thou hast been honorable, and I have loved thee: therefore will I give men for thee, and people for thy life." [God calls them,] "my jewels," Mal. 3:17.

[He] sets an higher value on the least and meanest {of the righteous}, than on all {wicked men}. He will destroy the wicked when they stand in the way of their welfare. Prov. 21:18, "The wicked shall be a ransom for the righteous, and the transgressor for the upright." He will deliver his saints out of trouble, though in order to it thousands of wicked men be brought into trouble by it. Prov. 11:8, "The righteous shall be delivered out of trouble, and the wicked cometh in his stead."

[God places] higher value on {the least of the righteous}, than on the greatest princes that are natural men; and therefore if any of them stand in the way, {God will not suffer them to touch his saints}. Ps. 105:12, "When they were few in number; yea, very few, and strangers in Canaan."

He that touches God's saints, touches "the apple of his eye," Zech. 2:8. Matt. 18:6, "better were it for him that a millstone were hanged about his neck, and that he were drowned in the depth of the sea." Yea, God will destroy whole nations. Is. 43:3–4, "For I am the Lord thy God, the Holy One of Israel, thy Savior: I gave Egypt for thy ransom, Ethiopia and Sheba for thee. Since thou wast precious in my sight, thou hast been honorable, and I have loved thee: therefore will I give men for thee, and people for thy life."

---

31. JE deletes: "*Obs.* 8. Hereafter God will gather the righteous unto him as a precious portion."

When the wicked of the old world were ready to swallow up the church; when the army of the five kings [took Lot, Abraham's son, captive, Gen. 14:12]; when the Egyptians [threatened the Hebrews at the Red Sea, Ex. 14:26–28]; when the people of Sihon and Og [opposed the Hebrews, Num. 32:33]; [when] the inhabitants of Canaan [opposed them]; when the great city Babylon, and the mighty Babylonish empire [captivated them: God destroyed them].

Yea, such is the value God has for his saints, that the whole course of nature {has been overturned on their account}. All things are theirs; all things are ordered for them. II Cor. 4:15, "[All things are] for your sakes."

God's value for his saints is either:

[(1)] That which consists in his love of benevolence. This is from eternity. From this, God has done infinitely greater things than to rebuke kings, {or to} destroy nations, {or to overturn the} course of nature: [God has] given his own Son {for his saints}. Or,

(2) There is that value which God has {for his saints}, consisting in his love of complacence, whereby he delights in the beauty he has put upon them, either by imputation or sanctification.

2. The saints are God's portion. This God often declares. Deut. 32:8–9, "When the Most High divided to the nations their inheritance, when he separated the sons of Adam, he set the bounds of the people according to the number of the children of Israel. For the Lord's portion is his people." [God] has as it were left the rest of the world to other gods. The great Creator and sovereign Proprietor of all has as it [were] chosen and measured out a particular part, that he reserves for himself, leaving the rest. Ps. 4:3, "the Lord hath set apart him that is godly."

Of old, God laid claim to a part of the produce of the fields of the children of Israel; and his part was the first fruits. Jer. 2:3, "holiness to the Lord, the first fruits of all his increase." Jas. 1:18, "Of his own will begat he us with the word of truth, that we should be a kind of first fruits." Rev. 14:4, "The first fruits unto God and the Lamb."

When it is represented that the saints are God's portion, it is not intended that they are the only part of the lower creation that has a right to, or the possession and disposal of [it]. [They are not] possessors of heaven and earth. He don't relinquish his right to the rest of his creation. [He] don't alienate his sovereign right to, and dominion over, wicked men.

But the following things are implied in the saints being God's peculiar portion:

(1) They are his in a peculiar manner, as they are those that God has chosen and called for a special relation and peculiar interest.

[1.] Relation.

[2.] Nearness.

[3.] Interest.

(2) They are his in a peculiar manner, as they are chosen and set apart for his special use, in a special manner, for his glory. "I have created him for my glory" [Is. 43:7]. [They are set apart] for a more honorable and excellent use. II Tim 2:20, "in a great house there are not only [vessels of gold] and of silver, but also of wood and earth; and some to honor, and some to dishonor."

(3) As they are that part {of mankind} that God has chosen and set apart for his delight. Ps. 135:4, "For the Lord hath chosen Jacob unto himself, and

Israel for his peculiar treasure."

[The saints are] God's food. Matt. 3:12, [God's] "garner." [They are God's] harvest. I Cor. 10:17, "one bread." "Good figs," Jer. 29.

[They are God's] spouse. Is. 62:5, "rejoice over thee as the bridegroom." Cant. 4:9, "[Thou hast] ravished my heart, [my sister, my spouse]."

[They are God's] orchard of pleasant fruits, Cant. 4:13. "[My beloved . . .] feedeth among the lilies," Cant. 2:16.

He delights in the saints in two respects:

1. In communicating himself to them. Jer. 32:41, "Rejoice over them to do the good." [The saints are] vessels of mercy. [God] delights in communications of himself, and his own happiness. Judgment is "his strange work" [Is. 28:21].

2. [God] delights in beholding the beauty that he has put upon them.

*Second* [*Prop.*] As the righteous are[32] God's precious portion, so he will hereafter deal with them as men are wont to deal with[33] that which they prize as the portion they live upon.

For the right understanding of this, I would observe,

32. MS: "of."

33. MS: "with as."

1. *Negatively.* This is not to be understood as though God depends on the saints, or any of his creatures, for any happiness. But,

2. God, from the great value he sets on the saints, of his sovereign pleasure and free goodness, will hereafter deal {with them} in many respects as {his precious portion}.

Though God is absolutely independent, yet he is pleased to set an high value [upon the saints]. 'Tis otherwise with God than with creatures. The value creatures set on things, is very much from their emptiness and indigence. {But the value} that God sets {on things, is very much} from his abundance. Such is that value that God, through this overflowing fullness, sets {on his saints}, that it is in some respects above all the value that men set on {things}. And he will hereafter treat {his saints as his precious portion} in many respects.

[I will] mention two or three instances:

(1) He takes thorough and effectual care of them, that none of them be lost. Thus men are wont {to take thorough care of} those things that they highly value, as those things that they place the happiness of their lives on.

(2) He will gather them and bring them home to him, to his own house. The husbandman with great care [gathers his harvest to his garner]. The merchant with great diligence and art gathers home treasures from distant parts of the world. So God gathers in his elect, and brings 'em home to him. Matt. 24:31, "And he shall send [his angels with a great sound of a trumpet, and they shall gather together his elect from the four winds, from one end of heaven to the other]." Eph. 1:10, "that in the dispensation [. . .] he might gather together in one all things." Hence the whole number of the saints are called by the name of the church, the "great congregation" [Ps. 22:25; 35:18; 40:9–10].

There is a twofold gathering in and bringing home of the saints to God: one is by effectual calling, the other is by bringing them home to glory. The greater part {of the saints are} gathered home one after another at death, but the universal ingathering will be at the end of the world, all in soul and body. God will then bring home his saints to his own house, as the husbandman {gathers his} harvest {and brings it home} to his garner. [The souls of the saints will be] brought to heaven, that is especially the house of God. There those jewels shall be laid up as it were in golden cabinets, precious and glorious repositories.

(3) [The saints shall be] laid up out of the way of all harm.

[1.] Storms.

[2.] Vermin.

[3.] Thieves.

[They shall be] infinitely above the reach of all.

(4) He will as it were thenceforward solace himself in them, as the husbandman, after he has gathered in, enjoys and makes use [of his harvest]. God will then fully answer the purpose of his grace, in the use that he will [make of his saints. He] will fully manifest his love. They shall fully enjoy God. The union and intercourse shall be perfect. They shall perfectly answer their end in glorifying {God}. God's complacence will be perfect. Zeph. 3:17, "The Lord thy God in the midst of thee is mighty; he will save, he will rejoice over thee with joy; he will rest in his love, he will joy over thee with singing." His inclination to communicate {his happiness and love}, will be perfectly gratified. [God will have] perfect complacence in the beauty [of the saints].[34]

## [DOCTRINE RESUMED.]
## OBSERVATION IX.

*God will hereafter cast away unsound professors.*

[Unsound professors shall be] "cast out, and trodden under foot" [Matt. 5:13].

*First.* He will discover them, as to any special interest or relation.

Some he will confess [that he knows them not], Luke 12:8, Rev. 3:5. Matt. 7:23, "I will profess [unto them, I never knew you]." Matt. 25:12, "Verily I say unto you, I know you not." Luke 13:25–27, "[When once the master of the house is risen up, and hath shut to the door, and ye begin to stand without, and to knock at the door, saying, Lord, Lord, open to us; and he shall answer and say unto you, I know you not whence ye are: then shall ye begin to say, We have eaten and drunk in thy presence, and thou hast taught us in our streets. But he shall say, I tell you, I know you not whence ye are; depart from me, all ye workers of iniquity]."

34. JE had later inserted a reference to Zeph. 3:17 earlier in the paragraph without deleting this earlier one. The top of L. 8v. JE headed "Application" and began to write a Use of Examination, and then deleted it, apparently deciding to treat Obs. VIII and IX in one Application. What was most likely the seventh preaching unit ends here; the next preaching unit begins on L. 9r. of this booklet.

*Second*. God will openly show that he has no value for them, and no delight in them. God don't [but] deal thus with false professors in general in this world. [They are called] reprobate. Jer. 6:30, "reprobate silver [shall men call them, because the Lord hath rejected them]." I Sam. 2:30, "[they that despise me shall be] lightly esteemed." Dan 12:2, "[And many of them that sleep in the dust of the earth shall awake, some to everlasting life, and some to shame and] everlasting contempt." Matt. 5:13, "[Ye are the salt of the earth; but if the salt have lost his savor, wherewith shall it be salted? it is thenceforth good for nothing, but to be cast out, and to be] trodden under foot." Mic. 7:10, "[Then she that is mine enemy shall see it, and shame shall cover her which said unto me, Where is the Lord thy God? mine eyes shall behold her: now shall she be trodden down as the mire of the streets]."

*Third*. He will cast 'em away, as he will no more improve them to any honorable use or purpose.

*Fourth*. They shall be visibly[35] removed as it were to a great distance from God. Ps. 101:7, "[he that] telleth lies shall not stand in my sight." II Kgs. 23:27, "[I will] remove Judah out of my sight."

[They shall be] driven away. Prov. 14:32, "[The wicked man is] driven away in his wickedness." Job 18:18, "[He shall be] driven from light unto darkness." Luke 13:28, "[There shall be weeping and gnashing of teeth, when ye shall see Abraham, and Isaac, and Jacob, and all the prophets, and you yourselves] thrust out." Rev. 3:16, [God will] "spew them out of his [mouth]."

*Fifth*. He will cast them away as to any regard to their welfare in this world. He will have no more to do with them in any way of favor. [He will] no more seek their welfare. [He will have] no compassion. [He will show] none of that care {that he has for the saints} towards wicked men while [they continue so. He will show none of that care towards wicked men], which [he shows] towards the brute creatures.

*Reason*. They are fit for nothing else but to be cast out and destroyed.

## APPLICATION.

[The] *Use* may be of *Warning* to all professors, to take heed that they ben't at last cast away.

35. MS: "visible."

There are no professors, whatever attainments in religion they are arrived at, and whatever evidences of their good effects they have, that are above such a caution. The apostle Paul did not think himself [above it]. I Cor. 9:27, "I myself should be a castaway." Therefore, let none slight this warning that is now given them, but take it as that which infinitely concerns them.

*First.* How many professors are cast away. There are multitudes of professors. Many seek to enter in. But Christ teaches [that the gate is strait that leads to heaven, Matt. 7:13–14]. There are many called, but few are chosen, as Christ teaches in another place [Matt. 20:16, 22:14]. All must appear before him whose eyes are as a flame of fire, and comparatively few will be then owned, and owned as some of those that are God's precious portion. There are many that have the charity and esteem of their neighbors, but God seeth not as man seeth. Luke 16:15,[36] "That which is highly esteemed among men is abomination in the sight of God."

*Second.* Consider what great disappointment the casting away of false professors will be attended with. False professors are like the foolish virgins [Matt. 25:1–12]. [They are] like the rich man [Matt. 19:16–24]. The day is coming when the wicked shall no longer stand in the congregation of the righteous, "but the way of the ungodly shall perish" [Ps. 1:5–6]. The dismal failing of the hope of the hypocrite, when called out of the world, is elegantly described. Job 8:11–19,

> Can the rush grow up without mire? can the flag grow without water? Whilst it is yet in his greenness, and not cut down, it withereth before any other herb. So are the paths of all that forget God; and the hypocrite's hope shall perish: whose hope shall be cut off, and whose trust shall be a spider's web. He shall lean upon his house, but it shall not stand: he shall hold it fast, but it shall not endure. He is green before the sun, and his branch shooteth forth in his garden. His roots are wrapped about the heap, and seeth the place of stones. If he destroy him from his place, then it shall deny him, saying, I have not seen thee. Behold, this is the joy of his way, and out of the earth shall others grow.

*Third.* If you at last prove to have been a false professor, you will see the privilege the true saints are admitted to, when you yourself are cast away. Luke 13:28–29, "[There shall be weeping and gnashing of teeth,

36. MS cites v. 14.

when ye shall see Abraham, and Isaac, and Jacob, and all the prophets, in the kingdom of God, and you yourselves thrust out]." Rev. 3:9, "to know that I have loved thee."

*Fourth.* You will then be more sensible of the worth of the privilege of such as are owned and treated as God's precious portion, than you are now. [You will] see how great God is. [You will] see all other things fail. [You will] see your need of God's favor. [You will see] what enemies and calamities you are exposed to.

*Fifth.* If the omniscient God, on your last trial, disowns you and casts you away, in vain will be your pleading former privileges and acquaintance. Luke 13:25–27, "When once the master of the house is risen up, and hath shut to the door, and ye begin to stand without, and to knock at the door, saying, Lord, Lord, open unto us; and he shall answer and say unto you, I know you not whence ye are: then shall ye begin to say, We have eaten and drunk in thy presence, and thou hast taught in our streets. She shall say, I tell you, I know you not whence ye are; depart from me, all ye workers of iniquity."

*Directions*

1. Don't cast away divine things as worthy of no value or regard. Don't cast God behind your back. I Kgs. 14:9, thou "hast cast me behind they back." Ezek. 23:35, "Therefore thus saith the Lord God; Because thou hast forgotten me, and cast me behind thy back, therefore bear thou also thy lewdness and thy whoredoms." [Don't] bid the Most High [to] depart from you.

[Don't] make nothing of his perfection, the revelations that he has made of himself, the instructions that he has given. Don't cast away God's love, and treat his holy communion as worthy of no regard. Hos. 8:12, "counted as a strange thing." Don't make light of God's honor and glory. Don't "make a mock at sin," Prov. 14:9.

Don't let Christ be a stone set at naught by you, and cast away. [The] builders cast away {this stone, which is become the head of the corner; don't cast away} his righteousness, Acts 4:11. Don't cast away the blessings of heaven.

2. Don't act as one that chooses distance and separation from God. Job 21:14, "Depart from us; we desire not [the knowledge of thy way.]" Job 15:4, "he casteth off fear."

3. Don't as it were cast out the Spirit of God.

4. Don't cast yourself away. [Don't] sell your soul for a song.

5. Don't live so as to be good for nothing but to be cast forth and trodden under foot, Matt. 5:13, as salt that has lost its savor.[37] "Wherewith shall it be salted?" [This] shows the more lamentable case of false professors than others. Take heed you ben't a barren tree in God's vineyard. [Don't] live without doing any good.

6. To your utmost, improve the day of God's mercy, while you are not as yet cast away.

7. See to it that you are upright in your profession, and in the duties you perform. Such shall never be cast away. Job. 8:20, "God will not cast away a perfect man."

Earnestly seek a better heart. Let that of the Psalmist, Ps. 19, three last verses, be your earnest and constant prayer: "Who can understand his errors? cleanse thou me from secret faults. Keep back thy servant also from presumptuous sins; let them not have dominion over me: then shall I be upright, and I shall be innocent from the great transgression. Let the words of my mouth, and the meditation of my heart, be acceptable in thy sight, O Lord, my strength, and my redeemer."[38]

## [DOCTRINE RESUMED.]
## OBSERVATION X.[39]

*God makes use of the ministry of angels in affairs relating to the eternal state of mankind.*

37. This leaf is made from a discarded prayer bid, which reads:

> William Clark desires that the y goodness
> of god may be acknolged in the congregation for
> his grate goodness to him in preserving him
> in his Absence from home an in recovring
> him from dangris sickness and in returing of him
> hom in safty and his parence desire ye same

38. What was most likely the eighth preaching unit ends here.

39. At the beginning of the preaching unit, JE recapitulates the text and observations covered thus far.

N. 6.                    June 1746.

---

Math 13. 47 ——- 50
obs. 1. like taking of Fish
2. – to all sorts
3. many seem to be Conv.
4. – not alw. enjoy their Elem.

[Angels are] made to be God's ministers, ministers especially to Christ in the great concerns of his kingdom. Therefore, [they are] all given to him.

[*First.*] What they don't and can't do, relating to the eternal state of mankind.

[*Second.*] Positively, how they are improved.

*First.* [*Negatively.*] What the angels don't and can't do, relating to the eternal state of mankind.

1. They could not have found out a way of salvation {for men}. Eph. 3:9–10, "[And to make all men see what is the fellowship of the mystery, which from the beginning of the world hath been hid in God, who created all things by Jesus Christ: to the intent that now unto the principalities and power in heavenly places might be known by the church the] manifold wisdom of God." I Pet. 1:10, "[Unto whom it was revealed, that not unto themselves, but unto us they did minister the things, which are now reported unto you by them that have preached the gospel unto you with the Holy Ghost sent down from heaven; which things the] angels desire to look into."

2. They can't purchase salvation for men.

3. They are not able to convert men.

4. [They] can't carry on the work of sanctification.

5. [They] can't bestow spiritual consolation, Christ's peace, joy unspeakable, [a] white stone, [or a] seal.

[They] may comfort, [as with] Jacob, Gen. 32, at beginning; [or as with] Daniel, Dan. 10:10–12.

6. They are not men's judges, authoritatively to justify or condemn men. They are not the searchers of men's hearts. [They] have no right originally vested [in them]. Nor has God given 'em authority. [He has] "committed all judgment to the Son," John 5:22; "and has given him authority to execute [judgment also]," v. 27.

---

5. not alw remain mingled.

6. This ☉ will come to an End

7. when the full number

8 – treat that which They

prize as the portion

9. —- cast away unsound

Professours

7. Nor can they be the authors of such a glorification or damnation as will be in another world.

*Second. Positively.* How God makes use of their ministry in affairs relating to the eternal {state of men}.

In general, {there is} no reason to suppose that all the ways are revealed. 'Tis not necessary for us to know.

1. God makes use of their ministry, in giving the means of grace. [He makes use of their ministry] in the communication of those revelations: particularly in giving the Law at Mt. Sinai, Ps. 68:17, Gal. 3:19. So, many of the revelations that were made to the prophets and apostles: Dan. 8:15, and chs. 10 and 11 and 12, 9:21, etc.; Zech. 1:9, 13–14; [and the] apostle John, Rev. 1:1.

And many of the particular revelations that God made from time to time to men, tending to their spiritual and eternal good, were made immediately by angels; as to Balaam, Num. 21:31, etc.; [to the] children of Israel, Judg. 2, at [the] beginning; to Zecharias, Luke 1; [and] to the shepherds, Luke 2; to Cornelius, Acts 10:3, etc.

[Angels are] assistants to the prophets and apostles in performing their work. [As] Elijah, I Kgs. 19:5, etc., "And as he lay and slept under a juniper tree, behold, then an angel touched him, and said unto him, Arise and eat. And he looked, and, behold, there was a cake baken on the coals, and a cruse of water at his head. And he did eat and drink, and laid him down again. And the angel of the Lord came again the second time, and touched him, and said, Arise and eat: because the journey is too great for thee. And he arose, and did eat and drink, and went in the strength of that meat forty days and forty nights unto Horeb the mount of God." [And] Peter, Acts 5:19, "But the angel of the Lord by night opened the prison doors, and brought them forth." Again, Acts 12:6, etc.,

> And when Herod would have brought him forth, the same night Peter was sleeping between two soldiers, bound with two chains: and the keepers before the door kept the prison. And, behold, the angel of the Lord came upon him, and a light shined in the prison: and he smote Peter on the side, and raised him up, saying, Arise up quickly. And his chains fell off from his hands. And the angel said unto him, Gird thyself, and bind on thy sandals. And so he did. And he saith unto him, Cast thy garment about thee, and follow me. And he went out, and followed him; and wist not that it was true which was done by the angel; but thought he saw

> a vision. When they were past the first and the second ward, they came unto the iron gate that leadeth unto the city; which opened to them of his own accord: and they went out, and passed on through one street; and forthwith the angel departed from him. And when Peter was come to himself, he said, Now I know of a surety, that the Lord hath sent his angel, and hath delivered me out of the hand of Herod, and from all the expectation of the people of the Jews.

[There is] no reason to think any other {assistance was offered to them, than is offered to} ordinary ministers.

2. The angels were improved as ministering spirits unto Christ, in the great work of obtaining our salvation. [They acted] as ministering spirits in introducing him into the world, in the revelation made to Mary, [and] afterwards to Joseph. [Angels were improved as ministering spirits unto Christ] in ministering to him in the time of his temptation, Matt. 4:11. [They ministered to him in the] time of his agony, strengthening him, Luke 22:43. [They were improved as ministering spirits at] his resurrection, [and] his ascension. [They are called the] "chariots of God" [Ps. 68:17].

3. [Angels are] ministering spirits to the elect in resisting and withstanding the evil angels that seek their destruction. There is a way maintained. Rev. 12[:7], "[And there was] war in heaven: [Michael and his angels fought against the dragon; and the dragon fought and his angels]."

Angels assist God's people against their temporal enemies. [As] in their wars with the Canaanites. Angels fought and assisted Deborah and {Sisera} against the Canaanites, Judg. 5:20. They fought from heaven.

Much more, [angels] assisted the human nature of Christ.

'Tis the angels that we must understand by the "valiant men." Cant. 3:7–8, "Behold his bed, which is Solomon's; threescore valiant men are about it, of the valiant of Israel. They all hold swords, being expert in war: every man hath his sword upon his thigh because of fear in the night.

4. In being the instruments of the preservation of the elect, till they are fitted for God's heavenly kingdom. Ps. 34:7, "[The angel of the Lord] encampeth round about." Ps. 91:11, "[For he shall] give his angels charge over thee." Thus the angels appeared for Jacob's preservation in time of great danger, Gen. 32. So at a time when general destruction was coming, {God instructed them} to set a mark {upon the foreheads of the elect},

Ezek. 9:4. So in Rev. 7, [at the] beginning, the angels are represented as holding back [the four winds of the earth]. The angels were made use of in the preservation of Lot, and so in the preservation of Elisha, II Kgs. 6:16–17. "And he answered, Fear not: for they that be with us are more than they that be with them. And Elisha prayed, and said, Lord, I pray thee, open his eyes, that he may see. And the Lord opened the eyes of the young man; and he saw: and, behold, the mountain was full of horses and chariots of fire round about Elisha."

5. The angels are improved as ministering spirits, to conduct the souls of the holy at death.

6. [The angels are improved as ministering spirits,] in separating the righteous from the wicked at the day of judgment. So the matter is represented in the parable {of the wheat} and the tares, Matt. 13[:24–30]. So in the text.

So that as the angels will be improved to conduct {the souls of the holy} at death, so it will [be] by their means {that the souls of the holy will} mount up at the day of judgment. They will then gather together the elect, Matt. 24:31. They will come with Christ from heaven to the judgment, to minister to him in the offering of the judgment. Dan. 7:9–10, "[I beheld till the thrones were cast down, and the Ancient of days did sit, whose garment was white as snow, and the hair of his head like the pure wool: his throne was like the fiery flame, and his wheels as burning fire. A fiery stream issued and came forth from before him:] and thousand thousands ministered [unto him]."

And this will be one way [the angels will be improved as ministering spirits].

7. They are improved to execute vengeance on ungodly men. [Angels are] often improved to this purpose in this world. Angels stood with a drawn sword to keep the way of the tree of life, Gen. 3:24. [They came to] Sodom, Gen. 19. [The destroyer smote the] first born of Egypt, Ex. 12:23. [The angel of the Lord] met Balaam, Num. 22:22. [An angel stretched out his hand] over Jerusalem, I Sam. 24:16–17. [Angels smote] the wicked inhabitants of Jerusalem, Ezek. 9:5–6; Sennacharib's army, II Kgs. 19:35; [and] Herod, Acts 12:23. Often in the Revelation, [they are depicted] pouring out the vials [Rev. 16:1–4, 8, 10, 12, 17]. [The angels' executing vengeance on ungodly men is] implied, Ps. 35:5, "let the angel of the Lord chase them."

So they will be improved at the day of judgment. Matt. 13:30, "Let both grow together until the harvest: and in the time of harvest I will say to the reapers, Gather ye together first the tares, and bind 'em in bundles to burn them." Vv. 41–42, "The Son of man shall send forth his angels, and they shall gather out of his kingdom all things that offend, and them which do iniquity; and shall cast them into a furnace of fire: there shall be wailing and gnashing of teeth." So in the text.

8. [Angels are improved as ministering spirits] in conducting the saints to heaven, when they shall ascend with Christ after the day of judgment. [They are called] "chariots of God" [Ps. 68:17], as attended Christ, and were as his chariots at his ascension.

So [it is] implied in [angels] being represented as the reapers [that] gather in God's harvest, gather the wheat into his barn, Matt. 13:30.

## APPLICATION.

*Use* [of] *Exhortation.* To seek the great privilege that they enjoy, who have the benefit of the ministration of angels.

*First.* How great is their privilege. How great a manifestation is it of the favor of God, the Creator of angels and men.

This will appear if we consider:

1. In what capacity the angels do minister.

[(1)] As the servants of their Redeemer.

[(2)] As their[40] angels. [It is] part of their inheritance, Matt. 18:10. "All things are yours," I Cor. 3:22.

2. What excellent and noble creatures the angels are. [They are called] mighty angels, morning stars, flames of fire, [and] thrones.[41] [They possess] superlative wisdom, [serve as] ministers of the court, [have] appearances like lightning, Matt. 28:4.

Fallen angels [are described as] roaring lions [Zeph. 3:3].

3. What benefits the saints have of the ministration of angels in this world. [They are] preserved in all their way. Ps. 34:7, "[The angel of the Lord] encampeth round [about them that fear him]." Ps. 91:11, "[For he shall give his angels charge over thee, to keep thee in all thy ways]." [Angels are improved] to help 'em against their enemies, temporal and spiritual. [They are a] glorious host. How great a privilege had Jacob.

---

40. I.e., the elect's.

41. II Thess. 1:7, Job 38:7, Is. 66:15, Col. 1:16.

How great a privilege [had] Elisha. [Angels stand about] the spouse of the antitype of Solomon, Cant. 3:7–8.

4. What benefits {the saints have of the ministrations of angels} at death.

5. How great benefits {the saints have of the ministrations of angels at the} day of judgment.

6. With what heavenly benevolence[42] and friendliness the angels will then minister to them.

[(1)] [They will minister with] delight.

[(2)] [There will be] joy in heaven.

7. Consider, if you are some of them, you will [be] like the angels. [The souls of the redeemed are] like the angels of God in heaven. Matt. 22:30, "in the resurrection they neither marry, nor are given in marriage, but are as the angels." Luke 20:36, "Neither can they die any more: for they are equal unto the angels."

8. You will have privileges above the angels.

*Second.* On the other hand, consider the misery of those who have no benefit of the ministry [of angels].

1. The angels will be executioners of God's judgments on them. It may be, in this world, [angels] may be a means of your death. [As the] sword of the destroying angels [I Chron. 21:12–16]. [You are] some of the same sort of men with these.[43] Ezek. 9:5–6, "smite: [let not your eye spare, neither have ye pity: slay utterly old and young, both maids, and little children, and women]."

However {the godly and wicked are mixed in this world, they will} certainly be hereafter separate. [Angels will] bind in bundles [the wicked, Matt. 13:30]. [They will be] cast into [the sea, Rev. 18:21].

They will triumph in your misery. Rev. 14:10, "in the presence of the holy angels." Rev. 16:5–6, "And I heard the angel of the waters say, Thou art righteous, O Lord, which art, and wast, and shalt be, because thou hast judged thus. For they have shed the blood of saints and prophets, and thou hast given them blood to drink; for they are worthy." Ch. 18:1, etc., "[And after these things I saw another angel come down from heaven, having great power: and the earth was lightened with his glory. And he cried mightily with a strong voice, saying, Babylon the great

42. MS: "Benevolent."

43. MS: "The at[?]," apparently a thought left incomplete by JE, or an intended deletion.

is fallen, is fallen, and is become the habitation of devils, and the hold of every foul spirit, and a cage of every unclean and hateful bird. . . . Therefore shall her plagues come in one day, death, and mourning, and famine; and she shall be utterly burned with fire: for strong is the Lord God who judgeth her]." Vv. 21–22, "And a mighty angel took up a stone like a great millstone, and cast it into the sea, saying, Thus with violence shall that great city Babylon be thrown down, and shall be found no more at all. And the voice of harpers, and musicians, and of pipers, and trumpeters, shall be heard no more at all in thee; and no craftsman, of whatsoever craft he be, shall be found any more in thee; and the sound of a millstone shall be heard no more at all in thee."

Then you will have none to pity you.

2. You will be delivered up into the hands of evil angels. It would greatly terrify you to meet the devil in the dark.

*Directions*

1. Avoid the ways of those who are set forth in Scripture, as those on whom angels have executed God's wrath.

[(1)] Sensual lusts. [As] Sodom.

[(2)] Obstinate. [As the] Egyptians.

[(3)] Self-exaltation. [As] Rabshakeh, II Kgs. 19:35, [and] Herod, Acts 12:23.

2. Seek an interest in Him who is the head of the angels. Come to mount Zion, to "an innumerable company of angels," Heb. 12:22.[44]

3. Strive to be more and more like the angels. [They are] flames of fire. The more you are like 'em, {the} more of their presence and assistance [will you have]. Men will the [more be their] delight. And the more will God employ them only in that service that is delightful to them.

4. Be evermore found in the way to heaven. 'Tis in this way. This is the ladder. As you would be found in the way to heaven, you must [strive]. Particularly,

5. Be evermore found in such ways, wherein we have an account, that Christ and his saints have had the benefit of the ministration of angels:

[(1)] Lot, [in] resisting the stream of general example.

---

44. See JE's 1740 sermon series on this text (*WJEO* 55, nos. 544–50).

[(2}] Jacob, [in] a secret converse with God, {and in a way to} wrestle with God.

[(3)] Elijah, [to] cleave to God in evil and degenerate times, [showing] boldness and zeal for the cause of God, I Kgs. 19:5.

[(4)] Christ, in resolutely resisting to temptation, standing fast and perseveringly through long-continued trials, suffering for others, wrestling with God for the good of others, {and} for the good of the church.

[(5)] Cornelius, in a way of almsgiving.

[(6)] Peter, [in] a way of suffering for Christ.

In the way of attending these directions, you will be in the way [of having the ministration of angels].[45]

### [DOCTRINE RESUMED.]
### OBSERVATION XI.[46]

*Wicked men will hereafter be cast into a furnace of fire.*

*First.* How they will hereafter be tormented with fire.
*Second.* How they are said to be cast into fire.
*Third.* How they will [be] cast into a furnace of fire.

*First.* How {they will hereafter be} tormented with fire.

1. The wrath of God, which they will suffer in their souls, is compared to fire.

2. Their bodies will hereafter be literally tormented with fire.

*Second.* How the wicked are said to be cast into a fire. Matt. 3:10, "every tree [which bringeth not forth good fruit is hewn down, and cast into the fire]." John 15:6, "[If a man abide not in me, he is cast forth as a branch, and is withered; and men gather them, and cast them into the fire, and they are burned]."

This manner of expression seems aptly to represent three things:

1. That God will subject them to their eternal punishment, with manifestations of contempt and abhorrence.

45. What was most likely the ninth preaching unit ends here.

46. At the beginning of this preaching unit, JE recapitulated the text:

N. 7.                July. 1746

Math 13. 50. 47 . ——— 50 . ———— and shall cast Them into a Furnace of fire.

2. That the wicked will be subjected to their punishment irresist-ibly, and sorely against their wills. [Whereas it is] said of the righteous, they shall enter [the gate of the Lord willingly, Ps. 118:20].

3. This naturally suggests their total misery. [They shall be] wholly miserable in every part, every faculty, every member, wholly swallowed up, full within, inward and without.

*Third.* {How they will be} cast into a furnace of fire. [It is] aptly represented as a furnace of fire, on two accounts:

1. {It is a place of} extreme heat.

2. {They are} shut up in a state of torment, as in a furnace. The fuel is shut in, as with walls.

[They are] imprisoned, enclosed in a strong vault, pent up.

## APPLICATION.

Let those consider it, who burn in the fire of lust, [or] secret wick-edness, [or] palliate their wickedness with {thoughts of their own self-righteousness}.

[The fire of God's wrath will] burn up your thin covering.

They that burn with the fire of envy, [will hereafter burn with the fire of God's wrath].[47]

[. . .]

6. Consider what fires the wrath of men have kindled.

7. Consider those fires that God has kindled, that have been en-kindled by God in the world, that have been signs of the fire [of hell].

[(1)] Sodom.

[(2)] Sinai, Deut. 5:4–6, "The Lord talked with you face to face in the mount out of the midst of the fire (I stood between the Lord and you at that time, to show you the word of the Lord: for ye were afraid by reason of the fire, and went not up into the mount); saying, I am the Lord thy God, which brought thee out of the land of Egypt, from the house of bondage."

8. What fires there are in the natural world, that may be looked upon as signs of the fierceness and dreadfulness [of the fires of hell].

9. What evidences have been of the dreadfulness of the spiritual fire of God's wrath on the soul, in the effects thereof in this world.

47. At this point in the MS, there is either a significant lacunae, or, less likely, JE in-serted the remainder of this preaching unit from elsewhere. L. 2v. of this booklet begins the Application up to this point, but L. 3r., also headed "Application," takes up with pt. 6.

10. Consider that the time wherein both your bodies and souls will be cast into a furnace {of fire}, will be a time wherein all things will be brought to perfection.

11. There will be great manifestations of the strength of God in that fire. Many expressions show it. Ps. 90:11, "Who knows the power of thine anger?" Ezek. 22:14, "Can thine [. . .] hands be strong, [in the days that I shall deal with thee?]" Heb. 10:35,[48] "[It is a fearful thing to] fall into the hands [of the living God]." Nah. 1:6, "Who can stand before his indignation? and who can abide in the fierceness of his anger? his fury is poured out like fire, and the rocks are thrown down by him." Rom. 9:22, "What if God, willing to show his wrath, and to make his power known, endured with much longsuffering the vessels of wrath fitted to destruction." Is. 33:10, etc., "Now I will rise, saith the Lord; now will I be exalted; now will I lift up myself. Ye shall conceive chaff, ye shall bring forth stubble: your breath, as fire, shall devour you. And the people shall be as the burnings of lime: as thorns cut up shall they be burned in the fire. Hear, ye that are far off, what I have done; and, ye that are near, acknowledge my might." "They shall know that I am the Lord."[49] II Thess. 1:9, "[Who shall be punished with everlasting destruction from the presence of the Lord, and] from the glory of his power." Is. 42:13, etc, "The Lord shall go forth as a mighty man, he shall stir up jealousy like a man of war: he shall cry, yea, roar; he shall prevail against his enemies. I have long time holden my peace; I have been still, and refrained myself: now will I cry like a travailing woman; I will destroy and devour at once. I will make waste mountains and hills, and dry up all their herbs; and I will make the rivers islands, and I will dry up the pools."[50]

### [DOCTRINE RESUMED.]
### OBSERVATION XII.[51]

*In the misery of the damned, there will be a mixture of sorrow and rage.*

48. MS cites v. 35.

49. Ezek. 28:23–24 and elsewhere.

50. What was most likely the tenth preaching unit ends here.

51. At the beginning of the preaching unit, JE recapitulates the text and observations covered thus far.

July 1746.

Math. 13. 47 —- 50 —— especially at this Time the latter part of v. 50. —— There

The future misery {of the damned}, is there[52] set forth by and represented by two expressions and manifestations of their misery: wailing and gnashing of teeth. Which seems to exhibit something diverse as to the inward cause. Wailing is an expression of extreme sorrow and grief; but here the wicked in hell are represented as expressing what they feel, and are the subjects of in the furnace of fire into which they are cast, not only by wailing, but gnashing of teeth.

Christ,[53] when speaking of the misery of the damned, was pleased often to represent it by such an expression of it, as Matt. 8:12, "But the children [of the kingdom shall be cast out into outer darkness: there shall be weeping and gnashing of teeth]." Again, Luke 13:28, "there shall be weeping and gnashing of teeth, when ye shall [see] Abraham, and Isaac, and Jacob, and all the prophets, in the kingdom of God, and you yourselves thrust out." Matt. 22:13, "Bind him hand and foot, and taken him away, and cast him into out darkness; there shall be weeping and gnashing of teeth." Matt. 24:50–51, "The lord of that servant shall come in a day when he looketh not for him, and in an hour that he is not aware of, and shall cut him asunder, and appoint him his portion with the hypocrites: there shall be weeping and gnashing of teeth." Matt. 25:30, "And cast ye the unprofitable servant into outer darkness: there shall be weeping and gnashing of teeth." So Matt. 13:42; so again in the text.

This representation that Christ so often makes of {the misery of the damned}, seems to be a signification of two things:

1. Extreme anguish, causing an universal, violent trembling and shaking of all parts of the body. Thus[54] in great fear and anguish of spirit,

shall be wailing & gnashing of Teeth ——

----

Obs. 1. – liking Taking Fish
2. To all sorts
3 many seem to be Conv.
4. – not alw. enjoy their El.
5. – not alw. remain mingled.
6. This ¤ will come to an End
7. when the full numbers.
8 – Treat that which They prize
9 – Cast away unsound professours
10. G. makes use of the minist of angels ——-
11. Herafter cast into a furnace

52. I.e., in the text of the sermon, Matt. 13:47–50.

53. MS: "X often when."

54. MS: "Thus sometimes in."

sometimes there will be that effect that was in Belshazzar: "Then the king's countenance was changed, and his thoughts troubled him, so that the joints of his loins were loosed, and his knees smote one against another" [Dan. 5:6]. And sometimes, under violent torment and anguish of mind, all parts of the body being put into a violent tremor and convulsion, the teeth will chatter and strike one against another from extremity of anguish. The word in the original[55] seems to signify any striking and grating of the teeth one against another.

2. Another thing that seems to be signified by this, is inward rage and fury. The expression of "gnashing of teeth" seems more generally used in Scripture to signify this. Job 16:9, "He teareth me in his wrath, who hateth me: he gnasheth upon me with his teeth." Ps. 35:15–16, "But in mine adversity they rejoiced, and gathered themselves together: yea, the abjects gathered themselves together against me, and I knew it not; they did tear me, and ceased not: with hypocritical mockers in feasts, they gnashed upon me with their teeth"; and 37:12, "The wicked plotteth against the just, and gnasheth upon him with his teeth." Ps. 112:9–10, "He hath dispersed, he hath given to the poor; his righteousness endureth forever; his horn shall be exalted with honor. The wicked shall see it, and be grieved; he shall gnash with his teeth, and melt away: the desire of the wicked shall perish." Acts 7:54, "When they heard these things, they were cut to the heart, and they gnashed on him with their teeth."

Hence the Observation that has been proposed as the subject {of this discourse}, seems justly raised from the words of the text, viz., that in the misery of the damned, there will be a mixture of sorrow and rage.

*First.* I would say something concerning the sorrow that they will be the subjects of it.

And as to the grounds of the future sorrow of ungodly men, I would observe in general that everything that they shall see, know, perceive, think or conceive of, will be an occasion of sorrow to them. Nothing [shall] afford any comfort. [There shall be] universal gloom, no gleam of light from any quarter. All objects and all things universally will conspire [to their misery]. Wherever they turn their eyes, [they shall find no relief]. Things past, present and to come shall all contribute [to their misery].

But more particularly,

55. נְתַנְשְׁדֵלֹט תִּ׃וּת סְמַֽנְֵרַב

1. The consideration of things past will fill them with sorrow. [The damned shall] remember things that are past. Luke 16:25, "Son, remember [that thou didst in thy lifetime receivedst thy good things, and likewise Lazarus evil things: but now he is comforted, and thou art tormented]." [They] shall be punished for their past sins, called to an account {for their past sins, and} judged {for them}. Ps. 50:21, "These things hast thou done, and I kept silence; thou thoughtest that I was altogether such an one as thyself: but I will reprove thee, and set [them] in order [before thine eyes]." As conscience will then be in perfect exercise, so will it be perfect in its reflections. [They would] gladly have their memory destroyed.

[The damned shall be] sorry for their past sins. [They will] vomit up their sinful pleasures. Job 2:12, etc., "[And when they lifted up their eyes afar off, and knew him not, they lifted up their voice, and wept; and they rent every one his mantle, and sprinkled dust upon their heads toward heaven. So they sat down with him upon the ground seven days and seven nights, and none spake a word unto him: for they saw that his grief was very great]." Prov. 23:32, "at last [it] bite like a serpent, [and stingeth like an adder]."

[They shall] bewail their folly, [their] misimprovement of time, [their] refusing to hearken to instruction. Prov. 5:11–13, "[And thou mourn at the last, when thy flesh and thy body are consumed, and say,] How have I hated instruction, [and my heart despised reproof; and have not obeyed the voice of my teachers, nor inclined mine ear to them that instructed me]!"

[They shall bewail their] past hopes and expectations, lament their past enjoyments; lament it that ever they enjoyed the gospel; lament it that ever they had outward enjoyment [of religion], that they lived so long [under it]; lament it that ever they were born. Job under his sorrows very pathetically cursed his day. Job, ch. 3, "Let the day perish wherein I was born, and the night in which it was said, There is a man child conceived. Let that day be darkness; let God regard it from above, neither let the light shine upon it. Let darkness and the shadow of death stain it; let a cloud dwell upon it; let the blackness of the day terrify it." But they [shall not be able to forget it].

[They shall] lament it, that ever Christ came into the world. What they will remember of the history of Christ, will occasion wailing.

[They shall lament] that ever God created the world.

2. They shall be filled with sorrow from things present. Everything that they shall see, or feel, or understand, that will then be present, [will fill them with sorrow]. [Their] souls [will be] filled with sorrow or suffering from the pains that will be inflicted on their bodies. Every part of the body will be an instrument and inlet of sorrow to their souls. All that they shall view or behold [shall cause sorrow]. They shall then see God; everything that they shall see in him shall occasion sorrow. What they shall see in themselves, what they shall see in their own bodies, [what they shall] see in their souls, [shall fill them with sorrow]. What they shall see in hell—devils, fellow damned men—what they will see of the place—full of nothing but dismal sights—what they will hear, [shall fill them with sorrow]. If they lift up their eyes to heaven, as the rich man in hell did, [they shall be filled with torment]. [They] shall [see] Abraham, Isaac and Jacob, [and all the prophets, in the kingdom of God, and they themselves thrust out," Luke 13:28].

Everything that they shall see or conceive of in heaven, what they shall see or conceive of in Christ then, all things that will be present, all their senses and faculties of understanding or perception, will be plagues to 'em.

3. The foresight and consideration of things future, will fill them with sorrow. [The damned] will know many things appertaining to futurity, and there will be nothing that they know of that will be future, or will in any respect have any expectation or imagination of, but what will be sorrowful. [They will] not be able to fetch one drop of comfort. Gladly therefore would they, if possible, be destitute of foresight.

Before the day of judgment, the wicked in hell will know that there is such a day is coming, and the expectation of it will cause sorrow in their hearts. The consideration of everything appertaining to that day will occasion sorrow. [They will] know that their souls will be reunited {with their bodies}. [They will know] all that shall pass with respect to them, all that shall pass with respect to the saints.

[They will have] the foresight of what will follow the day of judgment. [They will have] the consideration of things that will be to all eternity, the consideration of the eternal existence of God, the prospect of their own future misery, the consideration of their own future and eternal existence.

I come now to observe, in the

*Second* place, how rage will be mixed with the sorrow of the damned in hell.

1. All their lusts [and] corruptions will be in a rage.

The corruptions of men are principles of a very active, powerful, and violent nature. [These principles] oftentimes do dreadfully rage in this world. In hell, all restraints will be taken off. [The damned will be] wholly given up {to their lusts and corruptions}.

No means [will be] used, no hope to restrain [them]. [There will be] no mercies to watch over natural principles: no human law, no good example, no {good} counsels [or] reproofs.

The devil will be let loose, to blow up {lusts and corruptions} as much as he will. Their pride will be without restraint.

[Their] affectation of their own glory and exaltation, [their] disposition to exalt themselves against God, and to assume divine honors, [will be without restraint]. [The] image of the devil in this respect will be perfect. This lust will reign and rage in them.

There is no reason to think but that their lust after earthly enjoyments will be continued and enraged, for {they will have} no relish of any better good.

Their enmity against holiness will be enraged. [They will be] left to the power of temptation. [They will] be in circumstances that will tend to enrage. [The] devil will be let loose to blow up {their rage}.

2. They will be in a rage one against another. [There will be] no union, [but] perfect hatred. [They shall be] like firebrands. So [they shall be] the instruments of one anothers' torments. [This] seems to be implied, Matt. 13:30, "bind them in bundles [to burn them]"; and that, Jer. 13:14, "dash them one against another." [They shall be] like devils one to another.

[They shall be] enraged with their wicked companions for the injuries they have done them.

3. {The damned in hell shall be} enraged with the saints. [They shall] rage with envy. Ps. 112:9–10, "his righteousness endureth forever; his horn shall be exalted with honor. [The wicked shall] see, and be grieved; they shall gnash with their teeth." [They shall] rage with hatred. [They shall rage] with revenge [against the saints] for their rejoicing in God's justice in their damnation.

4. [The damned in hell] will rage against God. [Their] enmity against him will be enraged. This will be without restraint. [Their rage]

will be vastly irritated. They shall have those things in God, that were the foundation of their enmity represented in such a manner, and under such circumstances, as [to] vastly enrage. [They shall] have a vastly greater sight of those things in God for which they hated him: [his] holiness and hatred of sin, his justice in punishing. Before, [they] hated him because he threatened; but now {they hate him, because the} threatening [is] executed. [They will] know that God hates them, see and feel God's wrath. [This will] excite their fruitless wrath, a dreadful spirit of revenge, vastly heightened by despair. We have all reason to suppose that what is said of [the beast's kingdom], Rev. 16:10–11, will be true of all {the damned in hell}: [they] "blasphemed God because of their pains."

When the wicked shall see {their misery, and} shall feel [it], to what a dreadful height will this raise their malignity and malice.

5. They shall in some respect rage against themselves. Their consciences will be enraged against themselves. [They] will with great rage curse their own folly. [Their] conscience [will be] as an enraged viper, gnawing {upon themselves}.

[They will have] an inward flame raging.

[. . .]⁵⁶

## [APPLICATION.]

[. . .] the hell flames will rage. Who can conceive of the rage of those flames? And how fruitless will be their opposition? How much in vain is a great rage to fight with such flames. If a viper should be thrown into the midst of a terrible furnace {of fire}, how much in vain [is it for it to fight]?

God's wrath will as it were rage. Omnipotence will exert itself in fury. And to what purpose will [be their opposition]? I Cor. 10:22, "Do we provoke the Lord to jealousy?" Ezek. 22:14, "can thine hands be strong, [in the days that I shall deal with thee?]" Men, on the accounts of their enmity and malice, are compared to briars and thorns; but how much is it vain {to set briars and thorns against God}? Is. 27:4, "who would set the briars and thorns [against me in battle]?"

And indeed, the damned will not be able, with all their rage, to support themselves against the rage of devils. Nor indeed will they be

---

56. There is apparently a lacunae in the MS at this point; L. 9 of this booklet picks up in what appears to be the Application, specifically, the third subhead of the first Use.

able to support themselves against the raging accusations and remorse of their own consciences.

Men's consciences in hell will not only condemn their past sins against God, but they will not justify their present rage against God. [They will] know it to be unreasonable. So that their consciences will condemn [them].

There will be one kind of rage against another—an enraged conscience against the rage of their hearts—thus putting all into the greatest uproar. Then will the wicked be like the troubled sea when it cannot rest indeed.

*Fourth.* This sorrow and rage will increase one another.

*Fifth.* This wailing and gnashing of teeth will be constant.

*Sixth.* This sorrow and rage will be desperate.

*Seventh.* This wailing and gnashing of teeth will be endless.

II. Consider how different the state of the saints in glory will be. In them, instead of a conjunction [of] sorrow and rage mingled, there shall be perfect joy and perfect peace. Everything that they shall see or conceive of, shall contribute to their joy and delight. All {shall be} pleasant and delightful. [The] remembrance of things that are past will serve to excite their joy and gladness. Everything that is present [will excite joy and gladness]. [The] foresight of future things [will excite joy and gladness].

And instead of that hellish rage, an heavenly, sweet, inexpressible peace and love shall possess their minds. Lusts of wicked men, {their} rage {and corruption, will be} unrestrained {in hell}. But {the lusts} of saints [shall be] entirely passed away, and on the contrary, amiable and sweet grace [shall be] brought to the highest perfection. [The saints shall enjoy] sweet harmony throughout, ineffable tranquility, holy and divine union. [The] flame indeed will be vehement, but instead of spending their time in wailing and gnashing their teeth and blaspheming, they shall spend their time {in perfect joy and peace}. Instead of raging one against another, and enkindling and enflaming another like brands {for the burning}, they shall in sweet harmony, as one holy, beautiful society, to their utmost contribute to each others' happiness. [They shall] have joy without [interruption], brightness without any shadow, peace without any jar, love without any mixture of envy or jealousy. Their peace and rest, and their love and joy, will be without any interruption.

[Their peace and joy] will not be abated by any fear of an end, and will be actually endless. And not only so, but will be increasing to all eternity.

*For Direction:*

1. You must get that principle and foundation of this hellish sorrow and rage, which you brought into the world with you, mortified and removed.

You was born with that in your heart and nature, that is the foundation {of sorrow and rage}. There is the seed of this dreadful disease. The poison must be removed by regeneration, and sanctification, [by] the mighty power of God.

Your heart must be broken.

2. Come to Him that has borne extreme grief and suffered rage, that sinners might be free. [Christ has] borne extreme grief, suffered rage. [He has suffered] the fierceness of the wrath of God, enraged by the provocations of sinners. [He suffered] the rage of devils, roaring lions, hellish serpents, [and] the rage of wicked men.

3. If you would not have eternal sorrow and wailing now, avoid such things as the wicked in hell hereafter will bewail.

4. If you would not have eternal sorrows now, avoid sinful joys and pleasure. Joy [can turn] into heaviness. Prov. 14:13, "the end of that mirth is heaviness." Luke 6:25, "Woe to you that laugh now, for ye shall mourn and weep."

Avoid those pleasures that hereafter will bite like a serpent.

5. If you would not [have] eternal sorrow {hereafter, now} seek godly sorrow. Repent of your sins in season. Ps. 126:6, "He that goeth forth weeping, bearing precious seed, shall doubtless come again with rejoicing, bringing his sheaves with him." Matt. 5:4, "Blessed are they that mourn, for they [shall be comforted]." Luke 6:21, "Blessed are ye that weep now."

6. If you would not have eternal sorrow, {now} see to it that your religious joys are well-founded.

7. If you would not have eternal sorrow, now comply with the bitter and hard things. Philip. 3:10, "conformed to his death." Rom. 8:17, "if so be that we suffer with him, that we may be also glorified together." II Tim. 2:12, "[If we suffer, we shall also reign with him]."

8. If you would not have eternal rage and gnashing of teeth hereafter, mortify those things now whose rage torments the damned in hell.

9. If you would not have eternal rage in your heart, now get your heart calmed and sweetened with those principles that are contrary to rage. If you would not have sorrow and rage joined together hereafter, let comfort and love be joined together now.

You may, many of you, profess spiritual comforts, [but examine whether you have true comfort].[57]

57. At the end of the sermon, JE wrote an announcement for a "Meeting of Children."

# INDEX

www.ingramcontent.com/pod-product-compliance
Lightning Source LLC
Chambersburg PA
CBHW020211090426
42734CB00008B/1018